For my heroes,
Mum and Dad

Baby Nikki

Mini-me at two

At the Emmy Kids Awards

Me and Mum

The Three Musketeers

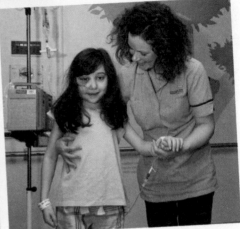

Recovering at hospital

Me and Dad

Happy birthday to me!

First published 2020 by Walker Books Ltd
87 Vauxhall Walk, London SE11 5HJ

2 4 6 8 10 9 7 5 3 1

© 2020 Nikki Lilly
With thanks to Siobhan Curham
Illustrations © 2020 Julia Broughton

The right of Nikki Lilly to be identified as
author of this work has been asserted by
her in accordance with the Copyright,
Designs and Patents Act 1988.

This book has been typeset in Futura and Likely

Printed in China

All recipes are for informational and/or entertainment purposes
only; please check ingredients carefully if you have any allergies
and, if in doubt, consult a health professional. Adult supervision
required for all recipes.

British Library Cataloguing in Publication Data: a catalogue record
for this book is available from the British Library.

ISBN 978-1-4063-9282-1

www.walker.co.uk

Nikki Lilly's
Come On Life

HIGHS, LOWS & HOW TO LIVE YOUR BEST TEEN LIFE!

WALKER BOOKS
AND SUBSIDIARIES

LONDON · BOSTON · SYDNEY · AUCKLAND

Contents

How did I get here?

Hey!

Thanks so much for getting my book. OMG, it still hasn't sunk in that this is my book! How crazy. I'm Nikki, but you may also know me as Nikki Lilly online! Up until the age of six, I lived a pretty standard life. My average day went a little something like – family, friends, school, repeat. I had so many passions and hobbies – everything from dancing to football. But then, when I was six, something happened that changed my life. I was diagnosed with an Arteriovenous Malformation (AVM). To put it simply, an AVM is when the blood vessels in a certain part of the body are incorrectly formed, which causes an enlargement of the veins, leading to swelling, pain and lots of bleeds. My AVM has caused one side of my face to change, which has been really hard for me to come to terms with. But one thing that I've learned is that even when life is incredibly tough, it doesn't mean you should give up on hope. In fact, I'm living proof that the very hardest of times can lead to the most magical experiences.

So how did I get here? After I was first diagnosed with my AVM, I felt quite lonely and isolated. I was spending all of my time at home as I had become very unwell. I felt really disconnected from the outside world and from other kids my age. I started watching videos on YouTube as a form of escapism, imagining myself as part of the vloggers' lives, like a friend. That's also when I started developing my passion for make-up, and one day I had the idea to film a video of my own. I put the family iPad on my dressing table and filmed myself rambling on about anything and everything I could think of. Little did I know that this would end up changing everything!

During my first year on YouTube, I posted generic videos like make-up tutorials and hauls because I thought that's what people wanted to watch. It took me over a year to get even 100 subscribers and I never got that many views, but it never mattered to me because I loved what I was doing.

One day, when I was ten years old and in Denver for medical treatment, I decided to film a video called "My Medical Story". Back then, I wasn't sure what to call it but that title just felt right, because that's what it was ALL about, sharing my story! Up until that point, my medical condition had been the overriding question on people's minds. I'd never talked about my appearance in my videos but I knew people would be wondering why I looked different and I thought it was super important to talk about it. If I had a video explaining my condition, then I'd be able to refer people to it and not have to keep explaining it and then I could move on. I also thought it'd help people understand and raise awareness. I tried filming that video so many times, but it never came out how I wanted because I didn't know what to say or how to say it. But, finally, I posted it.

The response from viewers was incredible and really helped my confidence. I was overwhelmed with all the messages of love and support; and loads of people – none of whom I'd met – said they'd learned from it, which was amazing! Their comments helped me to see myself for who I really am, instead of feeling defined by my medical condition. From that point on, my condition was just a part of me that I tried to embrace. I no longer let it control me or how I lived my life. It was amazing because that had never been the intention behind the video. I just thought I was making it in the hope of helping other people to understand, but it ended up helping me way more than I ever thought it could.

Another positive thing about that video is how it impacted my channel. Before, when I was focusing on fitting in and creating things I thought people wanted, the most views I'd get would be 2,000 per video. To date, my medical story video has got five million views, which is literally insane!

In 2016, when I was twelve, I managed to build up enough courage to enter a CBBC show called "Junior Bake Off". I definitely wasn't a baking pro when I took part in the show but, somehow, I ended up winning and baking became another massive passion of mine, and a form of escapism for me. After I won, CBBC asked me if I'd be interested in having a show of my own called "Nikki Lilly Meets", where I'd interview public figures about what they were like at my age. I love doing this and have met some incredible people along the way.

The idea of this book is to share with you some of the things I've learned over the years as I've grown up. Like everyone, I have bad days and good days but hopefully, if I share some of my harder times, it will help you feel less alone in yours. So, enough of me rambling! Let's get started...

"I'd rather be myself by myself, than be with someone I can't be myself with."

CHAPTER ONE
Be yourself

It's so hard to feel comfortable enough to be yourself, but being true to yourself and being authentic is one of the most important things when it comes to being happy. Sometimes it can be so hard, especially as a teenager. There's so much pressure on us to fake it to fit in and to present a glossy image of perfection to the world through social media or even in real life. One thing I've learned from the tough times that I've had over the last few years is how important your friends and family are when it comes to being yourself. My friends and family are my world; they help me be the best version of myself, and I don't know where I'd be without them. I probably wouldn't be on YouTube! They hold my hand through the bad days, and cheer me on through the good. They push me to do the best that I can, without pushing too hard. My parents are so supportive of me pursuing my dreams, and I'm lucky enough to be really close to my older brother and sister too.

The great thing about having a close family is that we're good at sensing if something is bothering one of us. When I'm having a bad day, my family can tell and always ask me what's wrong and if I want to talk about anything on my mind. They're so supportive and have helped me build my confidence. For example, when I get hate comments online – which make me feel pretty rubbish

– my family are always there to remind me that the person commenting doesn't know me and hasn't walked in my shoes, and the comments say a lot more about them and their unhappiness with themselves and their lives than it does about me.

Even if you don't get on well with your family, you can create your own little "family" of friends. I'm lucky enough to have a couple of friends who are so close to me that they're more like sisters. Here are some things that make me feel like my true self, and who knows, some of these might work for you too.

Do what makes you happy

Feeling like your true self can be as simple as doing something that makes you happy. I mean, I say simple … but sometimes it's tricky to find the thing that clicks with you. I was like that with the guitar in primary school. A lot of my friends were learning it, so I thought I should too because I was scared I'd feel left out. I had guitar lessons every week for nearly a year, but I just couldn't get into it. I tried but, after three months, I was still trying to learn how to play "Twinkle Twinkle Little Star" – out of time and off-key, may I add – and it was driving me and my parents crazy, so I decided to stop. You definitely need to connect with an instrument to be able to play it well and I, one million cajillion per cent, didn't connect with the guitar.

A couple of years ago, I bought a ukulele and I loved it! Even though it kept going out of tune as soon as I stopped playing it … or even while I was playing it, it definitely felt like a friend to me. For a start, it's a lot lighter than a guitar and only has four strings, so I instantly felt more comfortable playing it. I'd bought the cheapest ukulele I could find on Amazon because I didn't want to get anything expensive just in case I didn't enjoy it. I must have asked my poor dad to tune it about 100 times in that first week! But he was really supportive and patient, and encouraged me to keep going. I'm super grateful that he did because playing the ukulele has been the source of so much fun, expression and inspiration for me. So what I'm saying is, if you're interested in something like music but don't enjoy the first thing you try, don't give up on your passion completely.

JUST KEEP PERSEVERING AND GO FOR IT UNTIL YOU FIND THE THING THAT MAKES YOU FEEL INSPIRED AND, MOST IMPORTANTLY, HAPPY.

Singing with my ukulele is my happy place!

Find time

I'm lucky enough to spend most of my time with people who help me feel comfortable being my true self. In my case, it's my brother and sister, although there was a period after they became teenagers when they didn't really want to hang out with their baby sister. I can't think why they wouldn't want to play aliens with me?! But now that I'm a teenager and they're young adults, we've grown closer again, which I love. Don't get me wrong, we do argue, though!

My siblings

My sister, Tasha, is my best friend. My favourite thing to do with her is to go for a drive in the evening when everything is quieter. We blast music out at the highest volume and sing our hearts out, and chat about things we feel awkward talking about in front of our parents, like boys or worries. But don't worry, Dad, I don't have a crush or a boyfriend … yet! I can tell Tasha anything, and she gives me the best advice because she's quite a realist.

My brother Alex and I love going out for food, as we are both real foodies! It's so nice to use that time to catch up, as he's usually quite busy. Alex and I talk about everything, from what's happening in a TV show we're both watching to any worries that might be on our mind.

You might not have brothers and sisters but, if you do, it's really worth regularly making time to hang out with them. It can bring you closer together and create memories but, also, don't stress if this isn't possible. You might, like Alex, Tasha and I, grow closer together as you get older.

And you've always got friends. I love spending time with mine and I try to have regular sleepovers at my house, because you get to see a whole other side of your friends compared to what they're like at school, and it always brings you closer. I love doing fun things like photoshoots and spa days, and once my friends and I even did our own version of the TV show "Come Dine With Me". It was so good! We took it in turns to cook each other dinner. OK, some dishes were more than burnt – well, basically black – and others were not the prettiest, but making time to do fun things with the people closest to me really helps me feel like my most authentic and happy self. It's like the emotional equivalent of charging your phone!

Chat it out

In my house, you always know where my sister has been because she leaves a trail of evidence wherever she goes – we call it the "Tasha Trail". It can be anything from butter left out in the kitchen to her charger in the TV room, or her shoes in the hallway. Sometimes, clearing up after her is such a major task my mum and I will say, "I'll take this room and you take that room." In hindsight, she should do it herself, but it's so much quicker this way!

And speaking of my mum, and probably all mums for that matter, one thing that my mum unintentionally does is to ask me to do something that she knows I'll do eventually, but still can't resist reminding me about a million times! She's like a broken record that always seems to stop at, "Nikki, don't forget…" or "Nikki, you need to…"

If there's something that's been niggling you about one of your friends or family members…

> IT'S ALWAYS WORTH TRYING TO HAVE A CHAT WITH THEM ABOUT IT. IF YOU BOTTLE IT UP IT'LL JUST GET BIGGER AND BIGGER.

Pick a time to chat when you know you won't be interrupted, and they aren't about to rush off somewhere. Make sure you think about what you're going to say, and say it clearly, but try not to hurt their feelings too much either. It's hard to do both I know, but it does get easier as you chat – and the more you do it. Believe me, I've had some difficult conversations, but it's always better to talk about what's bothering you than to keep it in. Be realistic. Don't ask for things that won't happen. There's no point asking your mum not to be annoying and nag because, as we've already established, nagging is what mums do!

It's also really important to hear your friend or family member out and let them have their say too. Their feelings are just as valid as yours, and you need to acknowledge them and try to see their side of the story, even if you think they're wrong. Be honest, but listen too. Basically, I always try to treat them the way that I'd want to be treated.

When things get serious

Occasionally, things can get way more serious than someone being messy or nagging you. Sometimes I feel like my mum and dad have more troubles because of me and my health situation, which can really get to me. My dad is his own boss which is great when I'm in hospital because he can take time off when he needs to but, obviously, when he takes time off, it can affect his income. Sometimes I get worried about how much money we have, but when I do, I've learned not to keep it bottled up. I speak to my mum and dad about things that bother me, and ask them to be honest with me, which usually helps a lot. You can also speak to someone outside of the situation who is close to you or the person you're worried about. It'll really help your peace of mind to know what's going on, and you'll get some emotional support without burdening or worrying your loved one.

Say sorry

Let's face it – none of us are perfect. Sometimes it might be that you're the one who's being annoying and someone might end up approaching you. I used to have this habit of interrupting my mum when she was on the phone or speaking to someone in person. I didn't mean anything bad by it, I'm just such a chatterbox that sometimes I can't help myself and I'll jump in and complete her sentences. I didn't even realize I was doing it. Then one day, when my mum and I were in the car coming home from visiting one of her friends, she told me that I'd been interrupting her and that it was something that had been going on for a while. She didn't shout at me or anything, she just told me that it wasn't the polite thing to do, and made me aware I was doing it.

The first thing I did was say sorry. I know it can be really hard to say sorry to someone, which is kind of funny because it's just a little five-letter word! S-O-R-R-Y.

But I totally get it. Saying sorry can be scary because you're admitting you messed up and you don't know how the other person is going to react to it, and I myself can be quite stubborn. But as someone who has had their fair share of mess-ups, you just have to swallow your pride and do what's right.

I'VE LEARNED THAT A HEARTFELT "SORRY" CAN BE ONE OF THE BEST AND MOST MEANINGFUL THINGS THAT YOU CAN DO.

You're showing the person that you appreciate them and that you understand how they feel. I always try to say I'm sorry because I know I'm not perfect, and I try to learn from my mistakes. After my mum spoke to me, I made a mental note to try not to speak over her in future. This is another positive thing about admitting when you've messed up – it makes life so much easier because it stops people from being resentful and holding grudges. And one thing I've definitely learned is that life is WAY too short and precious for grudges – it's so important to talk things out because you never know what might be around the corner.

Be kind

I really believe that kindness is the most powerful thing that there is.

> I THINK KINDNESS IS OUR DEFAULT SETTING –
> BUT SOMETIMES THINGS CAN HAPPEN THAT STRESS
> US OUT AND MAKE US WANT TO CLOSE OFF.

I've experienced that first hand, but I also know that when you're kind to people, not only do they benefit, but you actually benefit so much too – if not more. Being kind brings you closer to people, and small acts of kindness go a long way, trust me. When my dad was unwell recently, my siblings and I made a big effort to try to be there for our mum by doing little things like unloading the dishwasher, tidying up, popping down to the shop to get something, and letting her know that we were there for her to talk to. It felt so comforting to be able to help her in any small way that we could.

Kindness truly is the gift that keeps on giving, and I think we should all sprinkle it wherever we go, like confetti!

Don't worry if friendships change

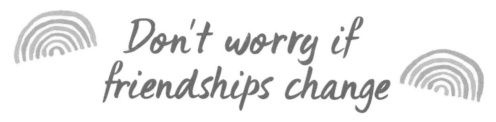

Sometimes you can naturally outgrow a friendship with someone who you were once super close to, and you feel like you can't be yourself around them any more. It can be really unsettling when this happens but it's OK and normal. Everyone changes so much as they get older; someone you might have had loads in common with in Year 7 might be very different by Year 9. I've had this happen to me a couple of times.

There's a girl that I was good friends with in Year 7 who I barely talk to now. Nothing bad happened, it was just that our personalities were very different and I felt like I couldn't be my true self around her. At first, it felt really awkward when we stopped hanging out together. We'd kind of avoid each other in the hallways at school because we didn't know what to say to one another, or how to say it. But then I messaged her and asked if we could have a chat, and we both had our say and it helped to clear the air.

Once we'd had that conversation, it felt quite natural to break away from each other, and on good terms. When I broke away from my friend, I asked other people if I could hang out with them at break and lunch. It may feel weird doing this but, genuinely, people really don't mind and eventually you will find a new friend or friendship group that you just gel with – like I have now.

Don't tolerate toxic friends

Toxic friendships are different to just growing apart from someone; toxic friends make you feel bad about yourself and have a negative impact on you. I haven't had a fully toxic friendship, but I know people who have, and how painful, uncomfortable and isolating it can be.

DO YOU HAVE A TOXIC FRIEND?

★ Do they make you feel insecure or uneasy?

★ Do they repeatedly hurt your feelings – and never acknowledge it and apologize?

★ Do they put you down or make you the topic of their jokes?

★ Do they regularly let you down and cancel on you without a valid reason?

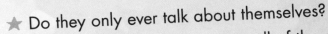

★ Do they only ever talk about themselves?

★ Do you feel like you're putting all of the effort in?

★ Do they try to manipulate your feelings or put pressure on you to do things that you don't want to do?

★ Do they speak about you behind your back and gossip about others?

★ Do they leave you out of things – in real life or on social media?

Toxic friendships can be hard to end, and this list might have made you realize that you have a toxic friendship that you need to break away from.

> IT'S ALL ABOUT TRYING TO LEAVE THE FRIENDSHIP WITHOUT MAKING THINGS WORSE OR CAUSING TOO MUCH DRAMA.

Try making yourself less available. Don't answer calls and texts as often you would normally. If you see the person in a class, try not to interact with them as much. Gradually slow things down. Don't give them mixed signals, make them aware that you're distancing yourself but not in a deliberately hurtful way. If you do have a conversation about going your separate ways, try to end things politely and wish them all the best. If you have mixed feelings about ending your friendship, it might help to write a list of reasons why the friendship isn't working or why it would be beneficial to your mental health to end it and then keep the list to read when you feel conflicted or guilty.

Now it's your turn!

And now I'd love it if you got involved. You didn't think you were going to get away with just reading, did you? At the end of each chapter, I'm going to set you a challenge so you can let me know how you get on via social media. For this first challenge, why not pick one of the tips I've shared in this chapter and try it out for yourself. Pick the one you feel you'll get the most from. And, remember, let me know how you do. Can't wait to see how it goes!

#COMEONREADER

"As long as you
can find one person
who really gets you
and cares about you,
it's all good."

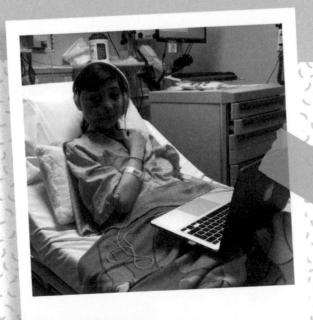

CHAPTER TWO
Find your way

I'm not going to lie – there have been times when I've really struggled to believe in myself, especially at school. I found my first year at secondary school so difficult because I didn't know anyone, and I was insecure about how I looked. I didn't have anyone to hang out with at break times or during lunch and I felt really left out listening to everyone else chatting and laughing in their groups. At the end of each day, I would get into my mum's car and start crying. I felt so alone; it was awful. But by the end of the year I began to find some friends and slowly but surely my confidence grew. This is about how I found my way and built my belief in myself.

Me and my besties!

Find your people

Because I look different, when I started secondary school, I found it really hard to go up to someone and start a conversation. I felt so nervous and self-conscious. Even if you don't have the same issues as I do, it's still really intimidating to go up to a total stranger and start talking.

> BUT NOW I KNOW THAT WHEN IT COMES TO MAKING FRIENDS — ESPECIALLY WHEN YOU FIRST START SECONDARY SCHOOL — YOU'RE NOT THE ONLY PERSON FEELING ISOLATED AND LONELY.

Most people are feeling exactly the same way too. All you need to do is take a deep breath, push out of your comfort zone, and have some questions at your disposal. I asked things like, "What's your favourite lesson so far?" or "Which primary school did you go to?" Whatever you ask, don't be afraid that they're going to judge you – chances are they'll be very grateful and happy you started a conversation.

In the end, I made friends by finding other people who were feeling left out. There were two people that I found myself sat next to a lot in different lessons and, although we didn't pluck up the courage to start a conversation ourselves, in the end we were kind of forced to when our teachers made us work together. Through our conversations in class I realized that they felt as lonely as me at school so, after a while, we started to have lunch together and our friendship grew. Another way I found my friends was by going to the library at break and lunch times. I used to go there a lot and sit on my own, then, one day, a girl came over and asked if she could sit next to me. We started having a conversation – obviously super quietly! We realized that we had lots in common. It was such a relief to not feel like I was the only one alone, and I felt hope that I could enjoy myself for the first time since starting school.

There are tons of ways to find your "people" at school, and I've found lots of friends through other friends too. But the one thing I've learned is that when it comes to friends, quality is definitely more important than quantity.

AS LONG AS YOU HAVE THAT ONE PERSON WHO REALLY GETS YOU, WHO CARES ABOUT YOU, AND WHO YOU CAN BE ONE HUNDRED PER CENT YOURSELF WITH, THAT'S ALL YOU NEED.

Join in

Joining clubs is another great way I've found to make new friends. The first club I joined was for creative writing. Then in Year 8, I joined the debate club. To be honest, I never would have joined if it hadn't been for a friend asking me to go with her, but surprisingly I really enjoyed it – and it ended up helping me with my confidence in social situations too. For the first three weeks, I'd just nod and would only say "yes" or "no" but as I saw the others standing up and speaking so freely, it made me realize that no one minded me being there or that I looked different, so it wouldn't matter if I voiced my opinion. And getting up to speak felt so empowering and liberating!

> I THINK CLUBS TEND TO BE MORE ACCEPTING THAN SCHOOL IN GENERAL BECAUSE YOU HAVE A PASSION IN COMMON, SO PEOPLE ARE MORE RESPECTFUL AND HAPPY TO GIVE YOU THEIR TIME.

And the great thing about clubs is that they make starting a conversation easier because most people have a lot to say about the things they love.

If there's a club you'd like to belong to but your school doesn't have yet, why not offer to start and run one? And if you're scared of going to a club on your own, you could ask someone else if they'd like to come with you, like my friend did.

Pack essentials

I always feel happiest when I have some of my favourite things with me (I mean, who doesn't?) and this totally applies when it comes to my school bag. For my first three years at secondary school, I had a backpack, but when I started Year 10, I decided to change it up a bit and bought a lovely big black handbag, which is super easy to hold and fits a lot in it. It's a bit like a Mary Poppins bag; I can shove everything into it from essentials to "just in case" items. As I'm sure you guys know all too well – when it comes to school, you need to carry so many things! Here's a handy checklist of my school bag essentials:

♡ **A CUTE PENCIL CASE** – filled to the brim with cute and quirky stationery.

♡ **A JAZZY WATER BOTTLE** – get a reusable one with a cool design on it.

♡ **A GOOD BOOK** – to help the journey to or from school go by in an instant.

♡ **PRACTICAL POPPER WALLETS** – great for keeping homework organized and clean!

♡ **NIFTY NOTEBOOKS** – I love "lil" notebooks – perfect for quickly jotting something down.

♡ **A SLIMLINE LUNCH BOX** – with lots of different compartments to fit all my lunch and snacks in.

♡ **MAKE-UP BAG** – packed with these go-to essentials:

- ♥ roll-on deodorant
- ♥ hand sanitiser
- ♥ lipbalm
- ♥ nude lipgloss
- ♥ concealer
- ♥ compact hairbrush
- ♥ travel size perfume (usually a rollerball)
- ♥ tissues

A SMILE IS THE BEST MAKE UP YOU CAN WEAR

Stay energized

OK, I know I'm stating the obvious here, but it's super important to eat healthily, especially for someone like me who needs to keep my energy levels up. With lots of late nights, early mornings and so much to remember, a good diet can make such a difference. Having said that, I also love sitting in bed, watching Netflix and eating my bodyweight in popcorn and anything I've baked! It really makes me sad when I see people my age stressing out about food and feeling guilty for eating something unhealthy. I think of my diet in an 80/20 split. As long as I'm eating healthily 80 per cent of the time, it's totally OK to eat less healthily for the remaining 20 per cent. All that matters is that you enjoy your food! Here are a few of my fave healthy snacks that help me to avoid the spikes and plummets that sugary snacks and junk food cause to energy levels:

♡ **HUMMUS** is super-filling and can be paired with tomatoes, carrot sticks or falafels – the options are endless. Just keep changing it up so that you don't get bored!

- ♡ **DARK CHOCOLATE RICE CAKES** are SO yummy and healthy too … what's not to like?!

- ♡ **APPLE SLICES DIPPED IN ALMOND BUTTER** – if you haven't tried it, you need to! GAME CHANGER.

Follow your own path

I was the only one out of my friends to choose Business Studies as a GCSE, but I really felt that I'd enjoy it and find it interesting. As someone who often feels left out because of the amount of time I have to take off school, this wasn't a straightforward decision to make, as it's always nicer to be with your friends in lessons.

BUT I REALIZED THAT IF I COULD SEE THAT A SUBJECT WOULD BE USEFUL FOR MY FUTURE, IT ONLY MAKES SENSE TO TAKE IT AND NOT BE SWAYED BY WHAT OTHERS WERE TAKING.

I didn't really know what kind of job I wanted to pursue when I was choosing my options, but I knew what I was interested in – YouTube, building a brand and working in TV – so I tried to choose subjects along those lines. I also had a chat with my sister, who had taken Business Studies before, to get a better idea of what to expect, which made me feel a lot more confident. I'm so glad I chose Business Studies, as it's become one of my strongest subjects, and I've found that sometimes not having my friends there means I can concentrate more in class. Plus, it also gave me the opportunity to get to know new people, which is a plus!

Don't stress exams

It's literally impossible NOT to stress at some point at school, especially when it comes to exams, but over the years I've learned to make some of the stress more manageable. I've definitely got a lot better at starting revision earlier. I always used to underestimate just how much time and effort I'd need to put into revision, and would end up having to pull an all-nighter to try to catch up. Now, I find that revision timetables are really helpful – there are lots of basic templates online – and super useful if you find it hard to plan and allocate your time to different subjects. I often procrastinate because I don't know where to start so I use revision guides to help me begin, and looking over practice papers nearer to the exam can be such a help too. The biggest stress is trying to remember all of the random things you need to know off by heart for an exam. Here are my favourite hacks that help me to memorize the info and facts you need to learn before an exam:

♡ **LETTER PATTERNS**: great for remembering words and people. Who remembers using "Richard Of York Gave Battle In Vain" to memorize the colours of the rainbow? Just make up your own sentences to memorize the first letter of key words/people.

♡ **READ ROBOTICALLY**: aha, OK, this is a weird one! I read over my notes then repeat them out loud – just to myself – really emphasizing each word. I know it sounds random, but it helps to embed them into your head.

♡ **MAKE IT FUN**: if I need to remember a lot of facts – like the order of Henry the Eighth's wives – I make up a story about them. For example, Henry the Eighth went to the shop, where he met (1) Catherine of Aragon, and then they went for lunch with (2) Anne Boleyn etc. If you can make subjects of any kind relatable in some way then you're likely to remember more. Now that's a fact. FACT!

The need to do well in my exams can make me want to revise for hours, but I've learned the hard way that it is SO important to take a break during revision. There's only so much your brain can take in! Taking a break also helps you feel refreshed and ready to come back to revision – just try and limit how long your breaks are, and don't disappear down a social media rabbit hole on a break! I like to go for a walk, have a coffee, or just sit in the garden to try to reduce stress. It also helps to get eight hours sleep a night, so that I wake up with a clearer head space.

Start and end your day well

I'm a big fan of a good routine to help me get my day off to a positive start, and chilling at the end of the day really helps me to make the most of it. Plus, I find that having a routine generally makes me feel happier because I feel like I've accomplished more and been more productive. Whatever your routine, it's so important to start and end your day well if you can. Here are some of the things I try to do:

♡ **GET GOING**: I find it really tough not to hit snooze on my alarm in the morning – who doesn't? – but once I'm up, I feel so much better, and waking up on time means I have more time to get ready, which always relieves some stress.

♡ **TAKE YOUR TIME**: there's nothing worse than feeling rushed in the morning! I like to take my time, have a hot drink and sort out my hair and make-up (if I'm going to wear it) – usually while having a little sing song – it definitely makes me feel more ready for the day ahead.

♡ **GET COMFY**: as soon as I get home from school, my first thought is to get comfy, have a rest and make a quick snack before doing my homework and having dinner.

♡ **GET SLEEPY**: my day normally ends with me sitting in bed with my laptop catching up on what's been happening online. Then I try to read a book just before I go to sleep – it's the perfect way to unwind and actually makes me feel more sleepy!

Now it's your turn!

Why don't you try to enrol in a club at your school or start a new one? This can either be for something you're interested in or something out of your comfort zone. I challenge you to go to a club you wouldn't normally dream of joining – like me and the debate club. Hopefully it will be surprisingly enjoyable for you too! If you do this challenge, I'd love to see the outcome for you on your social media – also, tag me so that I can congratulate you!

#COMEONREADER

YouTuber Saffron Barker

"Don't strive for followers; strive for happiness."

Talented make-up artist, Abby Roberts!

CHAPTER THREE

The world of social media

I love social media – which probably isn't a surprise to you if you follow me online!

> I THINK THE SECRET TO HAVING A POSITIVE ONLINE LIFE IS ALL ABOUT HOW YOU USE IT.

YouTube was the first social media platform that I started using and the thing I loved most about it was the interactivity of watching videos. I found it fascinating to be able to be a fly on the wall in someone else's life. Videos were a big factor in me building up the courage to start my own channel because I saw them as a way to connect with the outside world and people my own age. When I was ten, my parents allowed me to create an Instagram account, but for over a year I had it on a private setting and they closely monitored it. I only posted fun and positive things at first – like what I'd been doing with my friends or photos of new make-up and nail polishes – because that's what I'd seen others doing. I wanted to fit in and follow what was "popular" – not because I wanted to gain followers but because I wanted people to like me. But as time passed, I realized I needed to be more myself – more vulnerable and real – the true Nikki. I don't know about you, but I find scrolling through endless posts of seemingly perfect lives can really get me down and be quite toxic to my mental health. I didn't want to show that to other people, especially as my life isn't at all perfect. I thought it was really important to turn perfection on its head, so I started posting about being a kid constantly in hospital, taking people along with me to appointments, documenting the hard days too. I wanted my followers to have more of an insight into every aspect of my life, not just the edited highlights but the reality.

And I've learned a few hacks and tips along the way. Whether you're just getting started in the world of social media or you'd like to build a platform of your own, I hope these ideas might help you find your place in the world of social media and make your experience a positive one.

Don't mind me, on cloud nine!

Be real

In 2018, after I came out of a coma, I started to post about more serious topics. I hadn't posted for ages while I'd been in hospital, and I didn't really know what to say. I ended up filming a video for my channel that gave my viewers an update about everything that had gone on. I was so worried about how they would react. I knew they would understand as best they could, as my subscribers are amazing, but I also knew that it's really hard to know what to say in response to the things I was talking about. I decided to be completely honest with them, not trying to make light of the situation just to appear positive. It turns out that I needn't have worried because I ended up getting an overwhelming amount of support, with people telling me they were so happy that I was back and wishing me well. I was really touched by how kind they all were, like an extended family. The whole experience taught me how important it is to go deeper than before – a lesson that has become even more important to me as my platform has grown and I've become more well known. I want to make sure that people are aware that even though I get to do cool things and meet some incredible people and idols of mine, my life can be super hard too and that's the reality for many of us.

The irony about social media is that you can feel so much pressure to fake it to fit in, but that only makes it worse.

BEING REAL EMPOWERS OTHER PEOPLE TO BE THEIR AUTHENTIC SELVES ON SOCIAL MEDIA.

If you spend loads of time in bed with your PJs on, post about that as well as going out and getting dressed up. If you don't wear make-up some days, make sure that's reflected on your account.

THE MORE TRUE REALITY WE SEE ONLINE, THE LESS OPPRESSION WE'LL FEEL.

And it's really important to show the less positive things and hardships in your life. Don't worry that people's perception of you will change. If anything, it will only change for the better. In my experience, people appreciate it when you're real and they can connect with you on a deeper and more meaningful level.

Stay safe

When I first started my YouTube channel, my mum, especially, was unsure about me, eight-year-old Nikki, being exposed to the world, where people aren't so kind sometimes. She only allowed me to use it with the condition that she and my dad could look after it, and I had to make sure the comments were off. At the end of the day, I knew that my parents just wanted me to be safe and wanted the best for me, so I was happy to compromise and be mindful about what I was doing.

Now if someone makes comments or sends me messages that make me feel uncomfortable or upset, I block, report or delete them. I don't respond. There are so many weirdos out there! This is why I think putting your account on private is the best way forward. It filters through all of the weirdos, so that you don't have to! I also don't give out any personal info on my social media, like my address, pictures of the outside of my house, or my school uniform with the logo. In my YouTube videos, I share that I live in London, but I never film outside my house or on my street. A good test that I use before posting anything is to ask myself:

> WOULD I SHARE THIS INFORMATION WITH A STRANGER THAT I MET ON THE STREET? IF THE ANSWER IS "NO", THEN I DON'T PUT IT ONLINE FOR FOLLOWERS WHO ARE ULTIMATELY STRANGERS.

Make friends

I've made some amazing friends through social media.
When I started out, I'd watch YouTubers that I loved, who weren't too big, and decided to message a couple who seemed to have similar interests to me, or who I thought I'd get along with. I'm not going to lie, it was quite nerve-wracking but I kept thinking the worst that could happen was that they wouldn't reply, so it didn't feel like I had much to lose and they'd know that I loved their videos. And the great thing was, they did reply! They told me that they actually loved my videos too! Then we started chatting about YouTube and our lives and now, whenever we're at the same events, we make a point of finding each other to say hi.

The fact is, most of us are online a massive portion of our time so it makes sense to build a friendship group and support network on your social media too. There are so many genuine people online who are doing it because they love it. Reaching out to someone you like is as simple as DM-ing them and introducing yourself. When I reached out to other YouTubers, I said something like: "Hi, I'm Nikki, I also have a YouTube channel and just wanted to let you know that I love your videos. Would love to keep in touch. If not, it's totally fine, I just wanted to reach out and say hi. It's good to have a friendly face online!"

I like to comment on a photo or video before I message the person directly. I never spam them with loads of comments and likes, just make one really nice and genuine comment, and then leave it a couple of days before I DM them. And obviously it goes without saying that I always try to be mindful and stay safe online, and make sure I know the person is genuine before messaging. There are quite a few fake "catfish" accounts out there.

Katie Piper — good friend and anti-bullying activist!

Post on your own terms

At first, if I missed a few weeks – or even one week – of posting a video on YouTube due to my health, school or other life things, I'd feel guilty and annoyed with myself about it. And often, even if I didn't really have the time, I'd bang out a video because I didn't want to let people down. It was the same on my Instagram. Back in 2017, I posted so many half-hearted selfies that I knew I wouldn't look back on and like – because I felt the need to post something in order to keep followers engaged. But now, I'm more confident about posting less because I know people will understand that there's always a reason behind it.

POST WHEN YOU WANT TO AND ON YOUR OWN TERMS.

Also, quality is so much better than quantity. Now, I only post photos that I'm proud of and that represent "Nikki" rather than things I'll look back on and regret. For me, that means less posy, pouty pictures and more pictures with meaning and impact, like a post of me smiling, or a positive quote, or a life update. It's really important to post things that represent you and your life on your terms, when YOU want to. Obvs, it's totally fine to post the "posy" pics too, but there needs to be a balance, a happy medium.

Don't strive for followers, strive for happiness

I always had a goal number of followers on Instagram.
First, that goal was to reach 100, then it was 200, and
then 300. Though followers and numbers were never my
justification of continuing with what I was doing or showing
that I was doing well, I never felt fully satisfied or fulfilled
because I constantly felt I could do better and would keep
striving for more. It was the same on YouTube – I would
compare my number of subscribers with other YouTubers.

Sometimes, when you get lost in the never-ending sea
of comparison you start to wonder if it's even worth your
time and energy doing what you're doing, and if you start
to play the numbers game, it can be devastating if those
numbers start to fall. But that's all just part of the game.

Sometimes, even now, I'll post something I like and lose
followers. At first it's disappointing and I'll think to myself,
I love this photo, why don't they? But then I remember that
people are constantly following and unfollowing on social
media, and it really isn't personal, so I try not to take it
to heart too much. I still don't have a lot of followers on
Instagram compared to my YouTube, but I know now that

when I'm least looking for likes and followers, the better I'll do. I just try to enjoy what I'm doing and let the rest come naturally. I also try really hard to remember that social media is just one insignificant portion of my life in the grand scheme of things. At the end of the day, it's much more important to feel respected and validated by the people I know in real life, than striving to get people I don't even know to quite literally "like" me.

If you've found that the numbers are really affecting you, try putting your account on private. I have to have mine on public now, but if I had the choice I'd choose private because then you actually know everyone you follow and who follows you. When you know each other you can all support and inspire each other, and share positivity.

Every month or so I have a clear out to make sure that I'm only following people who have a positive impact on me and my mental health. For me, this includes people who post quotes about anxiety, for example. I also love looking at mindfulness/self-love accounts. I follow Katie Piper, LIZZO, Billie Eilish and Winnie Harlow, as they're such inspirations to me. I want to follow people who empower.

SOCIAL MEDIA SHOULD ADD TO YOUR LIFE, NOT TAKE AWAY FROM IT.

Don't let the haters win

I posted my first YouTube video in 2013, when I was eight. When I finally did turn the comments on, a couple of years later, the first comment I got that really upset me was something like: "You're so ugly. People are only watching you because your face is messed up." I've had a lot worse since then but hearing that as a ten-year-old was really hurtful. Actually, it honestly almost broke me. I'd only just about accepted the way I looked and it made me start questioning everything. I kept wondering why I had bothered starting a YouTube channel and thinking no one would be interested in what I had to say; that they'd all watch me to make fun of me, that they would pity me, that's why they would subscribe. I remember going downstairs and showing my parents. Straight away they told me to block and report the person. Then they gave me a meaningful pep talk, reassuring me that my feelings were totally understandable and valid, but I mustn't let the haters win. They explained to me that there are SO many people in the world that sometimes people aren't going to be nice, but if they're mean and hateful, it says much, much more about them and their own insecurities about themselves and their own lives, than it does me. It made me realize that I mustn't let this one comment stop me from doing what I love and what helps me on my bad days.

My parents also regularly remind me that if I find the negative comments hard to take, I can always turn them off for a while or have a break from everything, if that's what I want, which helps me to feel much more in control of it all.

Haters are really one of the biggest downsides to social media, but I'm determined not to let them beat me. Here are some tips I've learnt along the way for dealing with the haters:

♡ **IF YOU RECEIVE THREATENING MESSAGES** or comments, immediately block and report the account.

♡ **DON'T EVER RETALIATE** – however tempting it might be (trust me, I've wanted to).

♡ **IF WHAT THEY'VE SAID ISN'T TOO BAD** and you do want to reply, use it as an opportunity to educate them. Sometimes people will say "You're ugly" on my videos, and I'll reply with, "Thank you, that's so kind!" – and then I'll block them. I don't always respond though, because it really isn't worth the energy!

♡ **TAKE A SCREENSHOT** of the messages or comments to save as evidence. It's so, so important to do this, as sometimes these things can escalate.

♡ **IF YOU'RE BEING BULLIED** on your social media, it isn't something to be ashamed of. It's not your fault and it requires a lot of strength to get through it, so you should feel proud of yourself for trying.

♡ **TALK TO SOMEONE** about it immediately, even if it doesn't seem "serious" to you. You're never alone and it's good to confide in a parent, guardian, teacher or school counsellor you trust. Sharing your cyberbullying story is a really brave thing to do but it will make you feel so much better, trust me, and may even give others struggling the courage to talk about theirs too.

♡ **DON'T BULLY BACK**, it's very important not to sink to their level, no matter what's said, you're better than that.

♡ **IF YOU SEE SOMEONE ELSE BEING BULLIED**, don't feel scared to tell someone – you'd appreciate it if the situation was reversed. Report the account to the social media platform and if it's someone from your school, report it to the school. At the end of the day the more people who report it, the more the platform or school will take it seriously. No harm will be done to you, you're just acting on something that doesn't feel right and isn't OK and you can always ask your school to keep you anonymous.

life is more than a selfie

I love a good selfie, who doesn't? But it's also just as necessary to love how you look when you're not in front of the camera – and not using a cute filter! I totally get how hard it can be when you scroll through your feed and see nothing but flawless selfies, one after another after another. If you find that other people's selfies are getting you down, try looking in the mirror with no make-up on and repeating to yourself: "I am beautiful." I know it sounds weird and a bit cringe, and maybe cliché, and you probably don't want to do this when other people are able to hear (that would be slightly awks) but, trust me, it actually works. Also, mute the account(s) making you feel rubbish if you don't want to unfollow it. This handy option on Instagram has changed my experience COMPLETELY, and now I feel like I'm using it for the better.

 # Digital detox

Although social media can be loads of fun and super useful, there are times when it can be very stressful too. This is when it's good to have some downtime from all devices. When I'm in hospital, I try my best not to go on my phone because seeing 100s of people with what appear to be seemingly "perfect" lives really doesn't help my mental well-being – which is already quite fragile. I try to use the "downtime" setting on my iPhone, where you can schedule a time of the day when you're unable to go on any social media-based apps for however long you choose. It's so simple, yet so effective. When I'm having an OK day I schedule it for an hour's detox, but when I'm struggling I literally do it for a whole day.

> TAKING A DAY'S BREAK FROM SOCIAL MEDIA IS A BIT LIKE RECHARGING AND RE-ENERGIZING YOUR BRAIN.

When I unplug for a day or so, it feels like I've had the memory card in my head wiped clean. I find it gives me much more time for doing other stuff like...

- ♡ **TAKING A LONG BATH** – with a bath bomb and bubble bath, obvs!

- ♡ **BINGE-WATCHING BOXSETS** – something on Netflix, although I've literally binge-watched everything at this point.

- ♡ **READING OR LISTENING TO A GOOD BOOK** – usually fiction.

- ♡ **BAKING SOMETHING** not too time-consuming, like cookies or cupcakes.

Now it's your turn!

Why not share something on your social media that you've never shared before and wouldn't usually think of posting. If you post a lot of make-up selfies, it could be a selfie of you with no make-up on, no filter, nothing. Or you could share something different from your life, like going for a walk in your local park. It doesn't have to be anything crazy, just something different to give your followers a broader view of you and your life. And don't forget to tag me if you do, as of course, I would love to see it!

#COMEONREADER

Dad loves a make over!

"Realizing that you are enough is the first step to being truly happy."

CHAPTER FOUR
Be comfortable with who you are

Along with having to deal with my health issues, I've found growing up and becoming a teenager quite difficult – not only did it impact me physically but also mentally. But I know I'm not the only one struggling because growing up is hard and confusing. All of a sudden you're noticing all these things changing in yourself, your emotions and your body, and then it becomes way too easy to start comparing yourself to those around you, which is guaranteed to make you feel worse. I used to be so bad at this. I would constantly put pressure on myself, comparing myself to the other girls in my school who were pretty or popular or smart, the list goes on – and this just led me to put myself down. I still do, to be honest, but I'm not as bad as I used to be.

ONE THING THAT'S HELPED ME IS REALIZING THAT GROWING UP IS DIFFERENT AND UNIQUE TO EVERYONE, AND WE ALL DEVELOP AT A DIFFERENT PACE.

I was quite a late developer in my friendship group when it came to starting my period. I started when I was fourteen, which made me feel like the odd one out, but now when I get bad cramps that keep me up all night

– breathing through the pain – I'm like, ugh, why did I ever want to start in the first place? And I ask myself that same question every month. I can now see that starting at an earlier age isn't exactly all unicorns and rainbows either. It was probably really hard and confusing to be the first of your friends to start your period. I know someone who started in primary school, which must have been so isolating and scary. I can't imagine what it must be like to not know anyone else who's started and to not have any friends that can relate to you or feel like you can confide in about it.

Everyone's journey is unique to them. You may think that other people have better skin or are more confident and popular than you, but that's just how they appear on the outside – inside they may have more scars than you know. Ultimately, I think growing up is all about slowly growing to love yourself and being patient with yourself, as everyone's experience is different. I've had lots of challenges along the way and there are things that I've found on the journey that have helped me to cope. I hope they can help you too, so that you feel more comfortable in your own skin – whether that's mentally, physically, or both – and make the not-so-delightful process of growing up easier to get through.

Don't compare

I think Year 6 was the turning point for me, because that's when I found I was comparing myself to EVERYONE. At first I would compare myself to classmates academically, and even though my attendance that year was only about eighteen per cent because of my health, I would bring myself down over not doing as well as other people. The fact that they hardly ever missed school didn't matter. To this day, I still have to keep reminding myself that I've missed so many more lessons than others, I can't expect myself to do exceptionally in everything. It's like if I was running in a race and I'd been made to start a lot later than everyone else. How could I expect to win? I don't really have a fair chance. It's not that I'm competitive, or that everyone else was given a BIG head start, it's just that I want to try my best and achieve the most. But one thing I've learned the hard way, is that...

IT'S SO IMPORTANT TO BE MINDFUL OF YOUR PERSONAL CIRCUMSTANCES WHEN IT COMES TO COMPARING YOURSELF UNFAVOURABLY.

After a while, the comparison became more physical for me and I'd start beating myself up for not being as pretty or popular as other girls. If you can relate, it's super important to remember that you might not like the way you look but we're all capable of being beautiful. Someone can look STUNNING but be really toxic and ugly on the inside. A good personality and kind heart, as cringey as it may sound, counts so much more, especially in the long run. You were built the way you are for a reason and...

> **WHEN YOU START TO CHANGE YOURSELF, YOU START TO LOSE YOURSELF AND YOUR IDENTITY.**

It almost physically hurts when you don't get as much attention as others but trust me, there's so much more to life than school and looks. Every time you get a compliment from someone who knows you, keep it in your pocket for a bad day to remind yourself that you are a good person; you are worthy, important, powerful and unique, and so much more!

The best way I've found to counteract all of the comparison is to...

LOOK IN THE MIRROR FIRST THING IN THE MORNING AND LAST THING AT NIGHT AND SAY: "I AM ENOUGH".

I usually say it twice. Once normally and then another time with the words really emphasized. When I first tried this, I couldn't see how talking to myself in the mirror could possibly help anything – I actually started laughing about the fact that I was even trying it – but the more you hear something, the more you believe it – sort of like a rumour.

REALIZING THAT YOU ARE ENOUGH IS THE FIRST STEP TO BEING TRULY HAPPY WITH WHO YOU ARE AND ACCEPTING THAT YOU ARE YOU FOR A REASON.

It might sound super weird, I know, but trust me, it really works!

Be period ready

Before I started my period, there were a few signs that something in my body was changing. I'd feel a bit uneasy, have cramps and was generally moodier, but even though there were signs, it did come as a shock when it finally happened. Luckily, I was at home, but your period can start anywhere at any time and when you least expect it, so be prepared and stock up on supplies. Period tracker apps are super useful but you can't rely on them 100 per cent because your cycle can sometimes be a bit sporadic, so it's definitely a good idea to keep some pads in your bag, or if you're going out without a bag, tuck a pad in your pocket. I use pads because I don't need any more stress while I'm on my period, and I don't know about you but I get a bit scared at the thought of using a tampon! Like, what if it gets stuck? I would never know! I carry some mild painkillers on me too. I still get cramps but they help to dull the pain for a few hours.

I try to pamper and be extra kind to myself when it's that time of month. My go-to is a clay face mask and spot cream. During this period (ha-ha – pun not intended), I always run a bath – there is literally nothing better than a hot bath, with a bath bomb or bubble bath chucked into the mix. PLUS all of that while watching a movie, bingeing on a series or just listening to lots of my fave chill songs. (To be fair, I do this daily, ha-ha!)

I also do a social media detox because I always feel more vulnerable and emotional when I'm on my period, and seeing endless pictures of "flawless" girls and their "flawless" lives makes my "ugh, I feel really ugly" thoughts even more prominent. I also see comfort eating as something completely and utterly deserved, and needed, for having to have a period. Every. Single. Month. Obviously I still eat fruit and veg but if I want a chocolate bar, I have it and I don't let myself feel guilty! The way I see it, I'm only on my period for a week, and if I'm eating healthily-ish the rest of the month, then it's hardly going to do much damage.

Ride the rollercoaster

When I struggle with mood swings, I remind myself that the way I'm feeling is mainly down to my hormones. I'm not going mad, even if at times it can feel that way! One time – sadly this is a very true story – I can't believe I'm saying this but … I was watching "Peppa Pig" (don't judge me, it's still as iconic now as it used to be when I was three!) and the story was something about Suzy Sheep moving away. If you're a diehard "Peppa Pig" fan, you'll know that Suzy and Peppa had been friends since 2004 and this development almost destroyed me. This is so embarrassing but, I'm not kidding, I was crying my eyes out and all I could think was, "Oh my god, my childhood is over!" Luckily I was watching by myself in my bedroom. The sadness felt so real, but when I came off my period, all I could think was, "OMG, I cried at 'Peppa Pig', I actually cried at 'Peppa Pig'!"

So yeah, I have had my fair share of experiences because of good old hormones, but when I spoke to my mum and sister about it, they told me that they sometimes felt this way too. It was reassuring to hear that I wasn't the only one who felt more emotional on their period. And it was comforting to know that it's OK to have a bad day or week. It's something we all go through at some point, even if the picture painted on social media by others doesn't show that.

love your body

When I was twelve, there were some girls in Year 7 who had D-cup sized boobs, while I was at the opposite end of the spectrum. The first time I bought a bra, the shop lady serving me told me that they didn't have any bras my size and that I was "really quite small" for my age. I asked her what a usual twelve-year-old size would be and she told me at least an A-cup and that I was smaller than that. My confidence dropped after that day, as I hadn't a clue that I was smaller than everyone else my age up until then. I couldn't stop thinking about it. When I went to secondary school, I wore a bra that was a bit too big for me. Even though I'm not able to do PE due to my AVM, I'd go to the changing rooms with the rest of the girls to get registered and I'd see all these girls with much bigger boobs than mine, and curvy, hourglass figures. In my head I had a flat bum and a flat chest. It made me feel so self-conscious. But what I didn't realize at the time is that the girls with the bigger boobs were sometimes struggling too. The fact is, everyone's body is different and, although it's hard not to feel a bit left out in a group of girls if you don't look like them, it's good to remember that everyone feels that way at some point, even if it is for slightly different reasons.

Another thing that can cause stress is body hair. Yay – another thing to add to the mix! I never wax – it hurts so much I just can't do it – but I started shaving my body hair when I was fourteen. We live in a society where being completely hairless is seen as the way to be more attractive, but I really think it should be up to us. I don't shave my legs unless I want to, which tends to only be in the summertime. In winter and autumn, when my legs are covered nearly all of the time, I just don't think it's necessary. And for school I just shave the tiny amount of exposed skin in between my skirt and socks. I have saved so much time doing this instead of shaving my entire legs. Like, I reckon it must be months, if not years, of time I've saved and spent doing better and more beneficial things.

In the long run, when it comes to our bodies, it's so important to do things our way and to do what makes us truly happy and feels most comfortable. I really believe that the body you're in now, reading this book, is the one you're supposed to be in. It's OK to change the body that you came in – as long as you're doing it for no one but yourself!

Nourish and look after yourself!

Be a spot detective!

I used to have really bad skin (and sometimes still do) and when I had acne, it really got me down. It took away my love of make-up and any self-confidence that I had built up. Every time I applied concealer over the spots it looked awful. I had a lot of acne scarring and redness for a long time, and it took about a year for it all to calm down. However, one thing I did learn was that it's so, so important to think about different aspects of your life in general when you're trying to fix problem skin. Could there be other things, like an allergy or a diet, or even left over make-up residue that aren't helping?

I kept a food diary for a month, noting down everything I ate and any reaction after in my skin. I realized that when I had normal, dairy milk in my coffee it made my skin flaky and spottier, so I swapped it for oat milk. I also drank lots of water and ate healthily (as much as I could) and avoided touching my face a lot. I also had a good stripped back skincare routine and gave my skin some daily love and much needed TLC, changing up the products that I used until I found ones that worked for my skin's needs and problems. It has helped! But if you have already tried all of this and your skin still isn't playing ball, try visiting a dermatologist or your GP.

 # Express yourself

As I got older, so many of my friends started getting their hair dyed, but I wasn't allowed to because my parents made Tasha wait until she was fifteen and my mum said it wouldn't be fair to let me get it done sooner. Having my hair dyed was something I'd ALWAYS wanted to do. I wasn't the biggest fan of my natural dark brown hair because I'm pale, so it made me look very washed out. I wanted something warmer and more vibrant.

I begged and begged my parents, but my mum (TBH my dad didn't mind either way) wouldn't budge. But then, when I was thirteen, I got seriously ill and had to be put into an induced coma for just over a week. Seeing me that ill was a real eye-opener for my mum, and while I was unconscious she would sit by my bed and say, "Please wake up, I promise I'll let you dye your hair. Please wake up." I don't remember any of this but when I woke up, I was so happy when my mum told me. I was quite sick and looking forward to that was literally the only thing I felt excited about at the time.

I got my hair dyed the day before my fourteenth birthday, and it was the best present I could have asked for. It had been such a tough year, but with my new hair I felt much more optimistic and hopeful. I got it dyed rose gold, my favourite colour – surprise surprise! – and my confidence grew instantly. It really helped me to express myself and the rose gold tint warmed up my skin so much. Before I had my hair dyed, I created a Pinterest board and pinned loads of pictures of people with a similar hair colour to what I was aiming for, to help me picture what it would look like on me. Obviously my hair wouldn't look exactly the same as theirs, but my hairdresser and I still found it super helpful. I also made a board of the same colour hair in different styles – the options are endless – to have a guide. As you can tell, I love expressing myself through my hair, but my hairdresser gave me some tips that I still remember now:

♡ **WASH-OUTS OR SEMI-PERMANENT DYES** can be a useful way of testing a new colour before you go for permanent dye.

♡ **IF YOU DO GET YOUR HAIR DYED** make sure you go to a good hairdresser; there's nothing worse than your hair not looking how you hoped and there's no instant solution and no real way to hide it, especially at school.

♡ **USE HEAT ON YOUR HAIR AS LITTLE AS POSSIBLE** – it can dry out your hair and makes the follicles more brittle. If you use heat, always use heat protectant spray too.

♡ **DON'T WASH YOUR HAIR TOO OFTEN.** Try to only wash it every three days at most if you can as washing strips your hair of its natural oils and causes dandruff when done in excess.

Cope with crushes

Crushes are another massive part of growing up.
I've had my fair share of crushes over the years, and
I know I'm not alone. My first crush was when I was in
Year 3 and it was on a boy in my class. I'd always liked
him, but there was just one small problem – all of my
friends liked him too *face palm*! I was like, "Oh great,
thanks girls, I've got a one in five chance of success."
But even if I did get lucky, my friends would hate me,
and if one of them was successful, I'd probably hate her
for a little while too. It was all very cute and innocent.

As we get older, crushes become less black and white,
especially if you're not sure how the other person feels –
I don't know about you, but I have NO clue how to tell
if someone likes me. I once had a crush on one of my
really close guy friends, and didn't want to say anything in
case I lost the friendship. Personally, I think if you have a
crush on someone IRL you should tell them; you just have
to make sure you're OK with taking that risk. I mean …
to be honest, I'm not sure I could build up the confidence
to actually say it in person, but it can be easier if you
put a clever twist on it. If they act weird it's probably an

indication that they like you. And if they say they "used" to have a crush on you also, then they probably still do.

If your crush doesn't like you back it can be really hard to process, especially if you have to see them every day in school, or *shudder* sit next to them in a lesson. It's so important not to take it personally, and to move on and meet new people. Try something completely different, take on a new hobby and respect your crush's boundaries. Unfollowing them on social media, or muting their account can be a big help. Make a list of things you love about yourself (ask others too). This can help you come to terms with the situation. Practise some good self-care – pamper yourself and express yourself through something creative, whatever that may be for you. Remember, it's not you, it's them. It might be a cliché, but it's so true. There could be so many reasons why they said no. So put on your fave happy tunes and try your best to shake it off – ooh, that's a good song choice actually – and don't wait around for them either. Remember your worth.

Celebrity crushes

I don't have a crush on anyone at school at the moment, but I'd be lying if I said that I didn't have a celebrity crush – or two, or four or two hundred and one. Just joking, that would be slightly concerning! My first celebrity crushes were Justin Bieber; Zac Efron in *High School Musical*, specifically "3"; and Leonardo DiCaprio, specifically Leo in *Titanic*. But let's face it, who hasn't had crushes on them?! Now, I change my crushes all the time depending on what I'm watching on TV. The great thing about celebrity crushes is that you know that, realistically, the chances of you getting together with them are less than zero per cent, but a girl can only hope, right? It's so funny to daydream every time they pop up on your screen about what you would do for your dream wedding and what your non-existent children would look like. Right now, my crush is more like Romeo Beckham.

You don't have to be attracted to a celebrity to have a crush on them. I have a few celebrity women crushes that I really admire for their work. I love Selena Gomez – she is stunning and such a talented singer and actress. Her song "Kill Em With Kindness" is a fave. And I can't forget Ariana Grande. I think she's amazing, mainly because of everything she's been through. Billie Eilish, THE QUEEN, is another crush of mine; I relate to her music so much, even though I might not have been through the same things she has – her voice, her individual and iconic fashion sense, and how hard-working she is, is incredibly aspirational. I'm literally her number one fan. If I met her, my life would be complete! She's not afraid to say what she thinks, has been really open about her mental health struggles and has achieved SO much at such a young age.

Now it's your turn!

Why not try to say "I AM ENOUGH" every morning and night for the next month and then share with me on social media if it's made any difference. It may seem like a weird one, but please try it at least. I hope it works for you!

#COMEONREADER

"In order to get to
the rainbow, you have
to learn to dance
in the rain."

CHAPTER FIVE

Dare to keep going

I've had many highs and lows in my life, but the worst low was in 2018. I was on a trial drug for my condition, which was giving me every side effect you could possibly get, including achy joints and severe acne. I'd never really had a problem with spots before this, but my skin became so bad that even make-up couldn't disguise it. This affected my confidence and, to top it all, I started having a lot of nosebleeds because the drug wasn't working. In the end, my mum had to take me to hospital to have my blood count checked. When they tried to put in the needle, it was really painful and triggered a major nosebleed, which was awful. They did manage to take some blood but weren't able to keep the cannula in, so they needed to take me to a ward to insert a proper line. The trouble is, I've had so many punctures it's hard for them to find a good vein. While they were getting me ready for the line insertion, the nurses got my blood results back and discovered that my blood count had dropped to five – it should be around twelve. I started haemorrhaging, again out of nowhere, and so it went down to three. It was such an emergency that they had to take me down to the operating theatre in my clothes. In the end, they decided to keep me in a sleep-induced coma for eight days to help stop the bleeding and keep me rested.

When I woke up eight days later, I found it so, so difficult to get my head around everything that had happened to me. I thought I would be waking up after the procedure once they'd stopped the bleeding and expected to be on a normal ward until I recovered. Waking up on intensive care was really scary and so incredibly depressing. Most nights I couldn't sleep because I was riddled with anxiety and confusion. I think the most I slept while I was there was three hours. I was surrounded by severely ill children and, while I was there, the girl in the bed next to me – who I'd learned from her dad was a fan of mine – passed away. A baby on the other side of me, also in intensive care, passed away too. I had seen them as connected to me in that situation so, when they didn't wake up, it was incredibly hard to deal with and process. And as a result, I still suffer with PTSD from that experience.

After a day or two, I was moved to a normal ward, but I had to learn to sit up and stand without assistance and walk all over again, as I'd been virtually in the same position for over a week. I couldn't even move my head, so I needed help doing everything, even going to the toilet, and I felt as if I'd totally lost my dignity. This is so hard to deal with at any age but, as a teenager, I felt really self-conscious and had to be babied almost – it was horrible. You don't want people's help, but you need it. I also felt very isolated from everything – I was off school for six weeks, and I didn't know how to begin to describe what had happened to me to my friends. I ended up coming up with an excuse because I didn't want to relive the trauma or have to keep explaining it all – there was no short answer.

 I'll never be able to forget the experience, and my mental health has definitely suffered because of it. I'm so scared it will happen again, and I still can't process the severity of what I went through. The trouble is, there are so many things that can trigger memories. While I was in the coma, my mum and dad played me my favourite songs, which was a lovely thing to do, but now when I hear those songs, they take me straight back to that horrible time so I have to avoid listening to them. A lot of things have been tainted by the experience. If I smell an alcohol-based cleaning product, it instantly reminds me of intensive care so I avoid those things too. The way I see it is, there are certain things I can't control, like having to go into hospital, but being able to control other things makes me feel like I have some power in my life.

You might be able to relate to some of this, or something bad might have happened to you that has left you feeling anxious or down. If so, here are some of the ways that I get through it all.

let yourself have a bad day

One thing that really irritates me when I'm having a bad day is when someone tries to brush it away, or makes light of it by saying something like, "Oh don't worry, it'll get better." Some people can be quite insensitive and naive when it comes to mental health because they don't always understand. Sometimes the best thing you can do when you're having a bad day is to allow yourself to feel down or sad. You can't distract yourself 24/7, and I don't always think you should. Allowing myself a period of time to feel rubbish and not push how I'm feeling to the back of my mind, listening to my feelings and acknowledging that they are there, helps me to stay centred and not neglect my mental health. But, at the same time, I try not to give myself too long to think about everything or it can all become a bit much. Overall, it's quite useful to take time to think about why I might be feeling the way I am, or to talk to a friend or family member about it.

Exercise yourself calm

Although I'm not able to do a lot of exercise, I know that it can be really helpful for anxiety or depression. My brother's found that when he goes to the gym, it helps his mindset and anxiety. When my mum and dad were training for a marathon for my charity, she said that running massively helped clear their heads and focus on the present. I find walking, even though it can make me realize how unfit I am, is great because I can go at my own pace. Walking can also be a more social form of exercise and, if it's a sunny day, it's nice to get some fresh air.

Another form of exercise that helps with my mental health is yoga. I do the more novice and non-strenuous poses that don't cause much strain on my body and follow YouTube videos to do half-hour workouts. Yoga helps my mind to slow down so that I can think more clearly. It helps me get a better understanding of why I feel the way I do and, if I'm not having a bad day, it's a great way to keep feeling good!

Breathe

I really don't like being in crowded places, which is why I've never been to a concert because I try to avoid places that make me feel anxious or uncomfortable. One of the first times I had a panic attack was when I was in Oxford Street with my mum, in December, for some Christmas shopping. It was heaving with people, and the pavements are very narrow, so I kept bumping into people left, right and centre. I felt so claustrophobic and trapped; I felt like there was no escape and my body sort of went into fight or flight mode. This made me very anxious. I managed to hold it in while we were walking through the busiest bit but, as soon as we got out of it, I had a panic attack instantly. I began to hyperventilate; I wasn't breathing properly so I felt dizzy, and then I got really hot and shaky. It only lasted for about 10–15 minutes, but it felt like an eternity. My mum helped me by talking me through it, telling me to take deep breaths and taking them with me. She also calmed and centred me, keeping eye contact, so that I could focus on her and not what was going on around me.

Simple breathing technique

I find this breathing technique super helpful if I feel a panic attack coming on, or if I'm just anxious. With one of my hands, using my index finger, starting at my wrist, I slowly trace up to the top of my pinkie finger, breathing in slowly for a count of five. Then, keeping my finger at the top of my pinkie, I hold my breath for three. Then I breathe out slowly for five, moving my finger back down to the gap between my pinkie and ring finger. And then I repeat the exercise on each of my fingers and my other hand. The thing I love about this breathing technique is that you can do it anywhere because people can't really see what you're doing. It's great for pre-exam nerves, anxiety, or public environments and it helps to regulate your breathing and clear your head space.

Make time for TLC

Pampering myself definitely helps to calm my thoughts.
Here are some of my top tips for taking care of yourself
on a bad day:

♡ **MAKE SURE YOU GET PLENTY OF SLEEP** – sleep helps
strengthen your brain.

♡ **TREAT YOURSELF TO SOMETHING** – whether it's chocolate
or clothes or make-up.

♡ **PAINT YOUR NAILS** – or go and get them done.

♡ **WATCH YOUR FAVOURITE FEEL-GOOD FILM.**

♡ **GO OUT WITH A FRIEND** to the cinema or for a meal,
or just have a cosy night in.

♡ **WRITE A LIST** of all the reasons why you're proud of
yourself, however silly or small they may seem to you,
they are still something.

Practise inner peace

When I'm stressed out and anxious, mindfulness can help relieve stress and improve sleep. Often, I can't sleep when I feel uneasy so mindfulness is my go-to for these sleepless nights. I can just zone out, and everything around me becomes so still. My cousin Adam is quite spiritual and got me into it. Although meditation doesn't get rid of the cause of your stress, it's worth a try. Meditation and mindfulness also gives me more energy to take on the day, and can help reduce my anxiety. It gives me a greater understanding of why I might be feeling the way I am, which is important because I can so easily lose my sense of self when I'm going through tough times, or if I'm struggling with depression or having a wave of anxiety. Meditation helps me to stop and listen to my head, which you often forget to do when life happens.

If I don't have a lot of time I'll do a two-minute mindfulness exercise on an app like Headspace. It's actually crazy what a difference even a couple of minutes can make. When I have more time, at the weekend or on a day when I'm at home, I'll opt for YouTube ideas instead. I just search "meditation" or "mindfulness" or both and tons of options come up so it's almost effortless to find the one that's right for you.

When in doubt, chill out!

Help others

OK, this might sound a bit weird, but helping others is one of the best ways to help yourself too. Why? Because it's guaranteed to make you feel better in some way. When I was diagnosed, AVMs were rare and weren't really talked about online. And what was on the internet wasn't very representative – there was so much focus on the scary things, like bleeds leading to people dying. Right now there's no cure for AVMs, or alternative treatment to slow down the growth of them or shrink them, and I really wanted to change this. In 2012, I started the Butterfly AVM charity to help raise money for research into treatment and cures for AVMs, and to provide a support network and raise awareness for other sufferers and their families as AVMs can be really scary and unpredictable. Seeing the positive impact that the charity has been able to make has been one of the most rewarding experiences. Helping others through the charity has been incredible, especially when it comes to getting through a hard time. I also try to regularly give food to a food bank or just do a random act of kindness, like holding a door open for somebody, or even simply being there for others like your friends and family. It makes such a difference.

Speak up

If you're feeling low or anxious then it's ALWAYS a good idea to speak to someone about it. My friends and family are the people I talk to and they've helped me through some SUPER tough times. Sometimes, if I really want to express how I'm feeling but I'm not quite ready to talk about it, I find writing about my feelings can be surprisingly therapeutic. If I can't be bothered to do any writing, I've found doing a voice recording on my phone can be just as helpful. The thing I like best about this is that I can talk to my phone as if it's a person but it won't judge me – it sort of just listens. I did feel a bit self-conscious at first – just like I did when I first started talking to a camera for YouTube – but once I got over that initial awkwardness, it was SUCH a lifesaver. If I'm feeling self-conscious, I'll put my phone in the corner and speak to myself, saying things like: "Recently, I've been feeling really anxious. I'm not sure why. Maybe it's because of x, y and z." This provides an immediate release and feels just as good as talking to a person. And if you do want to actually talk to someone so that someone knows how you're feeling, but you don't want to tell them face to face, you can always play or send them the recording. Playing voice recordings back at a later date is a bit like reading an old diary – you can see how far you've come. Fingers crossed, it's a lot – and for the better.

Have an attitude of gratitude

I try to write down or think of three things that I'm grateful for at the end of every day. I like three because it's not too many if it has been a bad day. I either just think of what I'm grateful for, or I put them on the notes page of my phone. If I put them on my phone, I always date them because I like looking back on them. It's really nice to remember the cool things that have happened. If you're having a very bad day, it can be hard finding things to be grateful for, or to see the good, but even small things like, "I'm grateful and proud that I got out of bed today" are things that will make you feel better. Practising gratitude is such a great way of changing your thoughts and hopefully, during the rough times, the way you view your day-to-day life as a whole.

So grateful for my nanny!

Now it's your turn!

Why not try meditating? You can either find a video to help you on YouTube or try one of the mindfulness apps that I've recommended, like Headspace. Whatever you're going through, I'm proud of you for fighting hard to get through your day. I know it's tough, but know it will get better and your current situation isn't your final destination.

#COMEONREADER

"Happy memories help me get through my tougher days and remind me of all the good things I have in my life."

CHAPTER SIX

Have fun

Sometimes in life, you've got to take time to have fun and ENJOY yourself! Whether it's spending time with friends, treating yourself to a pamper day or just appreciating the simpler things in life, I always make sure to treasure the fun times that I have, and the happy memories that they create. They really help me get through the darker days, and remind me that there's always a light at the end of the tunnel.

Sometimes the simple things in life are the most valuable things. I've known my best friend, Leah, for years now, and she's become like a sister to me. Last year, when Leah had finished her mocks and I'd finished my essay deadlines, we decided to treat ourselves because we deserved it! Usually, we chill at each other's houses in trackies or PJs and binge-watch something on TV, but this time we decided to do something a bit different. We got dressed up and put some make-up on and then went out for dinner. Mum and Dad try to give me as much freedom as they can, but it's tricky because I could need medical attention at any time. Their letting me go to London for the evening without them was a massive deal. We got a taxi there and back to try and ease their worries and made sure I could contact them if anything happened. I chose the place we went to because they do the BEST Mexican food. It was so nice to go out and have that

extra bit of freedom with one of my favourite people. We ended up talking about everything from school and exams to silly things, like, you know, what we'd be if we were a vegetable. I think I'd be an asparagus or a mushroom. It depends on my mood, really. The best thing about our evening was that it wasn't extravagant, but we just had such a lovely time taking artsy Instas. I was able to forget about my health and just enjoy myself for an evening. These simple pleasures literally mean everything to me. The happy memories mean and count for even more when things get rough — they are there to look back on. I'm reminded of all the good things I have in my life. Here are my favourite things that I do to enjoy myself and escape. You can do them by yourself or with your friends...

Make it count

I really try to make the time that I have with my friends count. I love having sleepovers because they give you a chance to get to know a friend a whole lot better, and they can be so much fun. My friends and I try to stay up as late as possible, but usually end up falling asleep much earlier than we aimed for. In fact, we're such lightweights; we often fall asleep within fifteen minutes of starting a film! It's a major life goal of mine to reach twenty minutes! Here are some of my fave things to watch:

TV SHOWS

♡ "Friends"

♡ "Gossip Girl"

♡ "Glee"

♡ "The Great British Bake Off"

FILMS

PG

- ♡ All the *High School Musicals*!!
- ♡ *Mamma Mia*

12

- ♡ *The Hunger Games* – my faves are 1 and 2
- ♡ *Black Panther* (my fave Marvel film)

15

- ♡ *Bridesmaids*
- ♡ *Step Brothers*

I like having different little sleepover traditions with each of my friends. My friend Sarah and I like going to get pizza from the local Italian, and I always get a Hawaiian. Pineapple DOES belong on pizza – not up for discussion! After food, we walk to the corner shop to get some nibbles for the night and chat about things we wouldn't normally, like how we're feeling within ourselves. It's the perfect way, and a really great opportunity, to make you feel even closer to your friends.

Treat yourself

As you know, I LOVE baking and one of my favourite ways to treat myself is to make pizza from scratch. It's so much nicer to tuck into a pizza when you've seen the whole process and know what has gone into it – and to know that there are no nasty chemicals in the ingredients. If my friends are coming over, I'll make the dough beforehand and have all the toppings prepped and ready. When everyone arrives, we all gather around the table and each make our own pizza together. We always have music playing, usually something we can sing along to like ABBA, the Beatles or old JLS songs – got to say "Beat Again" is my number one GO-TO! – on our fave throwback playlist. The thing I love about our little pizza parties is that there are no time constraints really – we all sit around the table in my conservatory and chat away, pop the pizzas in the oven to cook, get them out – and time always runs away like that, which usually shows you're having a good time. Here's my recipe for raspberry mocktails which taste and look amazing, and make the perfect pairing for your pizza.

Raspberry lemonade slushy mocktails

INGREDIENTS
(MAKES 6)

- ♡ 600g frozen raspberries
- ♡ Juice of 3 lemons
- ♡ 225ml soda water
- ♡ 9 ice cubes
- ♡ 3 tbs runny honey

METHOD

1. Put all the ingredients in a blender or food processor (ask an adult for help if needed).
2. Blitz until a smooth slushy consistency.
3. Divide the mix between six cups, serve and enjoy (or store any remaining mocktail in the fridge).

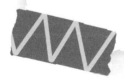

Do a DIY spa day

I love a DIY spa day – or night. TLC at any time is a good time. It can be the perfect way to unwind, relax and have some downtime with yourself or friends. These are some of my recipes for a non-expensive pamper:

Relieving under eye shadows

This is a perfect hack for those pesky "panda-style under eyes" you can get after late nights spent revising and early mornings getting up for school. This might sound really random but all you need are a couple of used tea bags, or two cold spoons!

THE WONDERFUL TEA BAG OPTION:

1 Cool two used black tea bags in the fridge.
2 Apply to closed eyes for 10–15 minutes.

THE GOOD OLD COLD METAL SPOON OPTION:

1 Put two teaspoons in the freezer for 15 minutes (in between some tissue).

2 Lay the rounded sides against your eyes for 5–10 minutes.

The moisturizing face mask

INGREDIENTS (MAKES 1)

♡ ½ avocado, mashed
♡ 1 tbs runny honey

METHOD

1 Combine the ingredients in a bowl.

2 Apply evenly to your face.

3 Leave on for 10–15 minutes.

4 Wash off.

The spot prone mask

INGREDIENTS (MAKES 1)

- ♡ 1 tbs runny honey
- ♡ 1 tsp turmeric powder
- ♡ ½ tsp sea salt

METHOD

1. Combine the ingredients in a bowl.
2. Apply a thin layer evenly to your face.
3. Leave on for 10–15 minutes.
4. Wash off.

The glowy mask

INGREDIENTS (MAKES 1)

- ♡ ½ banana, mashed
- ♡ 1 tbs of freshly squeezed orange juice
- ♡ 1 tbs runny honey

METHOD

1. Combine the ingredients in a bowl.
2. Apply evenly to your face.
3. Leave on for 15 minutes.
4. Wash off.

DIY Lip scrub

INGREDIENTS (MAKES 1)

- ♡ ¼ tsp brown sugar
- ♡ ¼ tsp runny honey
- ♡ ¼ tsp coconut oil

A SMILE IS THE BEST MAKE UP YOU CAN WEAR

METHOD

1 Combine the ingredients in a bowl.

2 Apply to your lips.

3 Gently scrub your lips in circular motions for 30 seconds – then wash or lick off!

Always do a patch test before trying new products! Apply a small amount to the skin on the inside of your elbow and wait 24 hours!

Get styling

I've never wanted to follow a crowd when it comes to my style and fashion choices, so I try to change it up from time to time. I've always been quite individual – sometimes quite edgy, sometimes quite colourful. Don't get me wrong, I totally get that it's really hard to be creative with your look as there's so much pressure to fit in, but it doesn't have to be all crop tops and high-waisted skinny jeans, you can find your own sense of uniqueness and style. Something I like to do that's a super simple way to be more creative is to buy something I've never worn before that's out of my comfort zone and pair it with an item I do feel comfortable in, like a pair of neon socks with my favourite black jeans. I'm all for slowly easing your way into trying new things and not doing anything too drastic at first.

Pinterest is a great outlet for fashion ideas and so is Instagram. I don't follow what I find to the exact detail, I just use it to get a different insight into how people dress and discover what feels interesting or exciting to me. YouTube is another great source of inspiration when it comes to finding your sense of style. I always search for things like "Cheap fashion hauls", "Cheap and easy styling tips" and "How to dress on a budget". The best thing is being creative through your look and the clothes you wear, and it doesn't have to be expensive. Reasonable high-street stores and charity shops can be good, and if you haven't had to break the bank on something, you won't feel like you have to wear it all the time, or feel restricted to that style.

Have fun with make-up

I feel like make-up used to be basic – a bit of eyeshadow and blusher and not much imagination – but now it's so much more exciting. It is literally an art form and I love how you can create any look you want, and be inspired by anything. Obviously I'm not a professional make-up artist, but I love being able to experiment and express myself. At the end of the day, what's the worst that can happen? If it doesn't look right, just keep trying and practising. Just like baking, practice makes perfect. Getting lost in creating a make-up look also really helps me zone out if I'm having a bad day. Instagram is one of my favourite places to go for make-up inspo; I always scroll through my favourite

make-up artists' feeds and think, "Oh my gosh, how did they do that???" But on a day when I'm not doing much, I love to attempt looks that I'd never wear out but that push me creatively and make me feel like my most authentic self. A good example of this is when I did a rainbow look for Pride – with all the colours of the rainbow! It took ages but it turned out so much better than I expected, and my followers, friends and family loved it. When you accomplish something you thought you never could, it makes it all the more special, and makes you all the more proud of yourself.

Now it's your turn!

Why not try a new look, or one of the recipes in this chapter and share it on your social media? Or you could share your favourite simple thing in life – the less extravagant the better! And don't forget to tag me if you do, as of course I'd love to see it!

#COMEONREADER

GBBO winner & JBO judge – Nadiya Hussain

"Growing in confidence is about being able to get back up and try again when you don't succeed."

CHAPTER SEVEN

Try something new

When I first applied to be on "Junior Bake Off" I thought I was OK at baking but I assumed that I wasn't good enough to get in. When I somehow managed to get through all three rounds of the entry process and was chosen – it was insane. I was so nervous about the challenges that they were going to set me, though I knew I could bake, I felt so anxious throughout the whole experience. I was sure I was sure I going to mess up – and better yet, mess up on TV!

The first "showstopper" challenge I was set was to bake and decorate an ombre cake. In case you didn't know, "ombre" is French for "shaded" (which I literally just found out) and it basically means something that has three or more different tones of the same colour. Thankfully, we were given our showstopper challenges in advance, so I was able to practise at home beforehand. The first time that I attempted to make one was NOT GOOD. It was actually awful. It tasted so sweet and looked BAD. I didn't have a clue how I was going to get from that to a decent showstopper that I'd be proud of. I actually started questioning and regretting applying in the first place. I ended up making about ten before the show. I was seriously that scared *face palm*! And, because I have this annoying need to always push myself I decided to do different flavours as well as colours. Oh, and to add a cherry on top – pun slightly intended – instead of making it three different flavours and colours, I had to one-up MYSELF and do four! I made it so much harder than it needed to be but, about six practices later, it all started to come together and my hope started to reappear. When it finally came down to the dreaded task of making it on the show, luckily, it was my best attempt of it yet. This was such an important lesson for me – I realized that whatever you're creating, there's always room for improvement, and the more you try, the better you'll get.

PERSEVERANCE AND DETERMINATION
EQUALS POSITIVE OUTCOMES.

I was really proud of myself, and thankfully all of the sleepless nights and time spent re-making and baking proved worth it. Timing had been a big issue for me, but everything just clicked and all the film crew watched mesmerized as I decorated the cake with the different shades of buttercream, from white down to pink. I could have built a whole house and stuck every single brick together with the amount of buttercream I made practising. I knew their reaction had to be positive, as the crew have probably seen so many cakes over the years, so that was really reassuring for me. Even when I did well, I always thought I was going home, even after my successful ombre cake.

> **SELF-BELIEF IS EVERYTHING WHEN IT COMES TO NEW EXPERIENCES AND CHALLENGES IN LIFE.**

Honestly, there are so many times when I have failed, and continue to fail, at things but I know now that this is a normal part of life. I've realized that there will always be someone who is better than me at something, but there'll always be someone not as good too. Just hang on in there and keep trying. The whole process of confidence and self-growth is about trying new things and being able to get back up when you don't succeed and trying again, and again, and again... And, you never know, you might end up accomplishing something amazing, just like I did on Bake Off!

Whisking the buttercream!

Get creative

It's so important to be open to new ideas and not let people, or things, in life shut our creativity down. I love writing and sometimes I write deep songs with lots of meaning or I mix it up and write about something light-hearted and fun – like hanging out with my friends or my love of baking or make-up. I might never use these songs or sing them publicly – fun fact, I get anxious singing in front of people. I have hundreds of songs that will probably never see the light of day – but either way, it doesn't matter because it really helps me creatively and mentally. You listening? Hey! OK. Good. Because I'm about to share a super useful tip – having a creative mind-set is a big part of succeeding in life – even in business.

If I get a creative block I try not to be hard on myself because that usually ends up making it worse. I always try to carry a notebook in my bag because I never know when inspo or an idea might strike and, in my experience, it's often at a really inconvenient time. You know, like in the middle of a Physics lesson, or while having a shower – ha-ha. Changing my location can also help massively counteract brain blocks. I find cafés and coffee shops are my fave places to go to spark my creativity – and not just because of the good coffee and cute aesthetic décor! Although, of course, that helps – not complaining!

Get writing

I really think that trying new things helps you to grow as a person. What worked for me was finding an easy challenge and having fun experimenting. That's how I discovered my love of songwriting. The first song I wrote was when I was eight years old. It was based on Taylor Swift's song "Love Story" – that song was iconic to eight-year-old Nikki – and when I say "based" I literally mean "copied", word for word. I mean, I changed some lyrics so I could say it was mine! When I sang it to my mum and dad they said, "Uh, Nikki, this sounds just like Taylor Swift!" But it didn't matter, you have to start somewhere, and everything in life in some way is inspired by something, or someone else. Using someone else's creation to inspire your own creativity can be a less daunting way of getting started, and can help you know where to start.

This might sound a little strange, but I write my best songs when I'm driven by an intense feeling, like depression or happiness. Basically, the stronger the feeling, the better the song, I find. In 2018 I wrote a song called "Feeling Blue" when I was feeling really depressed – and I wrote it in a record-breaking fifteen minutes! It was just me, sitting on my bed, crying, and I found myself drawn to my notepad. I picked it up and it all literally just poured out of me. It was after I'd been in hospital and I still wasn't well enough to return to school or press play on my average life. I decided that I'd just be vulnerable, be real and listen to myself and see what happened. If you put pressure on yourself creatively, or put a time limit on creativity, you'll always be stuck. It's so important to let your creations develop organically and authentically.

#CreateDontHate

Get baking

As I'm sure you're aware by now, I LOVE me some baking! The thing I love most about baking is the way you can easily improve at it. Even if you're rubbish at the start – if you keep trying and experimenting, you'll soon see improvements – it's all about development. And there are no boundaries when it comes to baking, decorating and flavour; you can literally make anything – OK not ANYTHING, but things within the realm of baking! I once made some cupcakes with a make-up theme and decorated them with little miniature lipsticks, palettes and eyeshadows made from fondant. It was so much fun. But if you've never tried baking before, here is one of the simplest recipes I know and it's perfect for a baking newbie: chocolate brownie in a mug – yes, you did read that correctly! As well as being simple to make, it's the perfect quick fix for a sweet craving and serves one!

Chocolate brownie in a mug

INGREDIENTS

- ♡ 2 tbs soft butter
- ♡ 2 tbs caster sugar
- ♡ 1 tbs light brown sugar
- ♡ 1 tbs cocoa powder
- ♡ 1 egg yolk
- ♡ ½ tbs vanilla extract
- ♡ 4 tbs self-raising flour
- ♡ Pinch of salt
- ♡ 2 tbs chocolate chips

METHOD

1. Put the butter in a mug and microwave for 10–20 seconds until melted.
2. Add both sugars and cocoa, then beat with a fork until combined.
3. Add the egg yolk and vanilla, beat together, then add the flour and salt and beat again until thoroughly combined and smooth.
4. Stir through half the chocolate chips.
5. Microwave for 50 seconds at 600W or 30 seconds at 800W or 25 seconds at 1000W.
6. Scatter the remaining chocolate chips on top and cook for an extra 30 seconds. Leave to cool – I usually leave it for 10 minutes – then enjoy!

Get online!

SUBSCRIBE

The internet is one of the best outlets for inspiration and expression, plus the best thing is, it's totally free! Two of my favourite sources of inspo online are YouTube and Pinterest (no surprises there – always talking about it on my channel!). Before I was diagnosed, dance and gymnastics were my two favourite forms of creative expression and both took place in classes outside my home or school. Having to give them both up after I was diagnosed was quite heartbreaking because I felt as if I'd lost part of my sense of self and my inner creative. So that's when YouTube became a lifesaver for me. It helped me find new things to fill the empty void of self-discovery in me.

Baking was the first thing YouTube helped me to explore and pursue after I got diagnosed. There are so many foodie YouTube channels, and it gave me that push to try things that were out of my comfort zone or that I'd never done before. At first my mum would help me a bit, you know, measure ingredients, put things in the oven etc., but then I started baking independently and attempting more challenging recipes, and it made me SOOOOOOO overjoyed. I was filled with happiness and rediscovery of things to fill my empty days with and to help release my creativity, while also helping to rebuild my confidence and redefine who I was.

So, the thing I love about Pinterest is that it gave me ideas for things that I would never have thought of on my own. When I decorated my room a while ago I wanted to try to have a really creative and different approach to the process, using a combination of my favourite prints and colours: marbles, rose golds and greys. The first thing I did on Pinterest was to create a board dedicated to my room, to give me an idea of what I wanted the overall vibe to be. Then, I started filling it with pictures and nifty décor hacks, because we LOVE a DIY job. I found an idea to use a hanging shoe rack on the back of your door to store nail varnishes as I have a huge collection of them – I'm talking every shade of every colour of every possible colour category! It was such an inexpensive and helpful way to colour code and store them in a way that I could easily see them, and didn't take up too much of my room.

Another cool creative hack I found on Pinterest was for an artsy, yet cheap, light. I literally just got a clear mason jar and put a set of fairy lights in it. Then I turned the jar upside down so the lid was on the bottom. It looked SOOOOO good, especially when I turned all of my lights off – it made little circles of light all around the room, which was surprisingly calming. I kinda see it as a nightlight, perfect for teenagers onwards!

Get crafty

Learning to make something homemade can be more fun than buying it and it's really satisfying – and sometimes therapeutic – especially when it's successful. It's also a great way to make personal gifts for your friends and family if you're on a budget. One of my favourite budget gift ideas, which I used to make LOADS of when I was younger, is make-up brush holder jars. You just get a clear mason jar – ha-ha, back at it with the mason jars – put a thin layer of glue on the inside and cover it in glitter. Then, when the glue is dry, spray the inside with hairspray to make sure the glitter sticks. I've done these in all different colours, from gold to pink to blue, and given them as gifts for birthdays and Christmas etc.

DIY pamper packs are another really sweet and thoughtful idea, especially as a "get well soon" or Mother's Day gift. I really like making face masks and lip and body scrubs, then I put them all in a gift box along with an eye mask and some thick cosy socks. Once, I wrote down 100 things that I loved about my mum and put each one in a separate envelope. Then I put them all together and gave them to her as a gift and told her to open one each day. This is a lovely present for someone who is going through a tough time. The things you write can be as simple as "I love how you always make me smile" or "I love your hugs". It's such a personal and heartfelt thing to do. You might see it as cringey and time-consuming but, honestly, this gift made my mum so happy, and it meant much more to her that I put so much time into it and that it was so thoughtful.

And then there's wrapping presents – full disclosure: I'm awful at wrapping. The award for WORST wrapper goes to – drumroll please *drums* – Nikki! Did you guess right? Nonetheless, I still try. Here's a cute example – at Christmas time I stuck a little wooden ornament and candy cane onto the ribbon around each of my gifts. If I have time, I also like to add a homemade card. One time I made a birthday card from a piece of folded brown card and I stuck a pink and white striped birthday cake candle on the front of it with double-sided tape, and then wrote "Birthday Wishes" underneath it, in what I tried to make look like a calligraphy style font. It was so simple but it looked great – the perfect combo!

learn life hacks

Life can be so busy, with so many different things to juggle, from school and homework to friends and family, and everything in-between, so I'm all about anything that helps to make things easier, not to mention cheaper! Here are some of my top life hacks to help you tackle some of the smaller – but still annoying and time-consuming – problems in life:

NO. 1 REMOVE STUBBORN STAINS: let's face it – stains only seem to happen when you're wearing your favourite outfit! But don't panic. Here are a couple of hacks for removing stains quickly, without having to change your perfect outfit:

♡ **INK STAINS:** apply a squeeze of hand sanitiser over the stain and rub with your finger until it's gone. Or rub some toothpaste over the stain and let it dry, then wash it off and leave to dry – it shouldn't take long.

♡ **MAKE-UP STAINS:** spray some hairspray onto the stain. After a few minutes, the hairspray should harden into the stain and the fabric. If this doesn't happen, spray the area again and wait another few minutes. Get a clean paper towel and run it under cold water – the colder the water, the better. Wring out any excess water and use the paper towel to blot the hairspray out of your clothing. Push down gently on the stain with the paper towel then lift it to see how much make-up has been removed. The make-up should come off along with the hairspray. Repeat until the stain has gone.

NO. 2 GET RID OF CREASES IN T-SHIRTS: There's nothing worse than quickly rushing to go out, putting on a cute outfit and then discovering that the t-shirt you're wearing is creased, BADLY. This is my go-to hack: smooth out the creases with my heated hair straighteners. Be careful though – you don't want to burn the tee – or yourself! I've got so many friends to use this hack too!

NO. 3 MAKE EMERGENCY MAKE-UP REMOVER: Coconut oil is a perfect emergency make-up remover, even if your mascara is waterproof or stubborn! Massage the oil into your skin and watch the make-up melt away, then wash it off with a flannel. This has the added bonus of leaving your skin super soft. But don't use it too regularly as it can clog your pores, and obvs nobody wants that.

Now it's your turn!

Why don't you start an inspirational or motivational Pinterest board for a passion you'd love to develop, such as dance, writing or art? Have fun finding, searching for, and collecting ideas and images for inspo in whatever you choose!

#COMEONREADER

"Keep trying
and you'll keep
improving."

Interviewing Mel C!

CHAPTER EIGHT

Be brave

After I won "Junior Bake Off", CBBC asked me if I'd like to have my own show with them called "Nikki Lilly Meets".
In each episode I interview a celebrity about their childhood and teenage years, and I put my own Nikki spin on it by baking each guest something that they'd try at the end of the interview. Even though I love presenting "Nikki Lilly Meets", when I first started I was really nervous, full of self-doubt and anxiety. It didn't help that the people I was interviewing were all public figures or celebrities. I kept putting them on a pedestal and believing that they were so much more than me. I was so scared doing my first interviews – and to make matters worse, I couldn't have any notes *nightmare* so I had to memorize all of the questions, which was really hard to do. But just like my cakes and make-up, when I look back on those first interviews, I can totally see how far I've come.

> IT JUST GOES TO SHOW THAT IF YOU REALLY LOVE DOING SOMETHING, YOU SHOULDN'T LET SELF-DOUBT OR FEAR WIN.

I'm so glad I didn't let fear make me want to give up on "Nikki Lilly Meets" – I've met so many interesting and lovely people who I've become friends with, and learned so many cool things about them all because of it. Here are just a few of the favourite people I've interviewed through the years, what I learned from them, and of course, what I've baked for them!

Stem ginger cake for Dame Jacqueline Wilson

(aka grandma goals/who I want to be my grandma)

Jacqueline Wilson was one of the first people I ever interviewed for the show, which was CRAZY because I'd been a massive fan of hers for years. I'm literally her number one fan! I've always found her books so relatable and have read all of them. I especially loved *The Mum Minder*, which is about a mum who is a childminder but has the flu and is looked after by her daughter. It was like the role reversal of my mum and me. I love how Jacqueline Wilson tackles important topics without hitting the reader over the head with them. *Girls Under Pressure*, which is about girls dealing with the way they look, is another favourite of mine. It's crazy because it was published back in 1998 before social media was even a thing and before those kind of pressures had grown to the level they are now. She really was ahead of her time.

> TO PUT IT LIGHTLY, I LOVE JACQUELINE WILSON!

I wanted to bake her something that was a classic but different at the same time, so I decided to make my stem ginger cake. I always love to make stem ginger cake, especially around winter time. It's a really comforting cake, you know *ooooh*, and I could imagine Jacqueline Wilson having a cup of tea along with it. It's a no-frills cake, but it has the best flavours. I interviewed Jacqueline Wilson at her house and she was so lovely and welcoming. After the interview finished, she invited us (my mum, Launa the producer, and me) to stay for some tea and cake, so I literally had to keep pinching myself that I was actually sitting with my childhood IDOL – drinking tea, eating cake and just chatting like normal. Like WHAT? I felt a real connection with her and I was so grateful and happy when she said, in a later interview, that I was her greatest inspiration and that she sees me like a granddaughter. I think she would make the best grandma ever; she's so lovely and so full of wisdom. Plus, you know, she'd never be out of bedtime stories! The highlight of my interview with her had to be when she said to me, "I don't think I've ever been given such a lovely cake." I couldn't stop smiling!

The most inspirational thing I learned from interviewing Jacqueline Wilson was when she told me about how difficult her home life was back when she was a teen. I love that she used her tough times to inspire her later

on, writing books about young people who are also going through difficult things – books which help them through theirs. Her books were a massive escapism for me.

Stem ginger cake recipe

This cake doesn't look like anything special but honestly, it IS very tasty!! Lovely to eat when it's cold outside...

- ♥ 250g self-raising flour
- ♥ 2 tsp ground ginger
- ♥ ½ tsp ground cinnamon
- ♥ 1 tsp bicarbonate of soda
- ♥ Pinch of salt
- ♥ 200g golden syrup
- ♥ 2 tbsp ginger syrup
  (from a jar of stem ginger)
- ♥ 125g butter
- ♥ 60g stem ginger
  (from a jar of stem ginger)
- ♥ 2 tbsp sultanas (optional)
- ♥ 125g dark muscovado sugar
- ♥ 2 large eggs
- ♥ 240ml milk

METHOD

1 Preheat the oven to 180°C (Gas mark 4). Line a 20cm square tin with baking paper.

2 Sift the flour, ginger, cinnamon, salt and bicarbonate of soda together.

3 Put the ginger syrup and golden syrup in a saucepan with butter and warm gently over a very low heat.

4 Finely dice the stem ginger and add to the butter and syrup mixture, followed by sugar and sultanas. Let the mixture bubble very gently for one minute, stirring occasionally so it does not stick.

5 Crack the eggs into a bowl and pour in the milk. Using a whisk, gently beat the egg and milk mixture.

6 Pour the butter and syrup mixture into the flour mixture and stir with a large metal spoon. Then add the egg and milk mixture and mix in until no trace of flour.

7 Scrape the mixture into the prepared tin and bake for about 24–40 minutes until a skewer inserted into the centre of the cake comes out clean.

8 Leave to cool in the tin and serve with either vanilla ice cream or custard.

Apple and blackberry loaf for Jamie Oliver

I chose to make my apple, blackberry and clotted cream loaf for my good friend, Jamie — you might know him as Jamie Oliver! I wasn't too nervous to interview Jamie because I first met him back in 2016 when he was one of the people who awarded me with a Pride of Britain award. I had no idea who was giving me my award, so when I saw that it was him, I was ecstatic! He asked me then and there if I'd like to do a collab and I was like, um, errr, YESSS!! Who says no to that? So we filmed a cooking video together in 2017 and I had the BEST time. He is such a lovely person and always checks up on me. Fast forward to 2019, when I interviewed Jamie at his HQ, we talked and laughed so much. He spoke to me about the struggles he has faced being dyslexic, what it's like being a (cool) dad of two teenagers – though he busted some dance moves which were pretty far from cool – and he spoke about his journey becoming a chef. Oh, and I can't forget when he talked about enjoying embarrassing his two eldest daughters and how he casually sharpens knives when certain boys come round. Ha-ha. It was so much fun – I wish I could rewind and do it all over again! When he tried my cake, he loved it so much that he called it peng. I mean … what more could you want than Jamie Oliver calling your cake peng? Not much that's for sure.

Since then, we have chatted lots and I actually was lucky enough to do my Year 10 work experience with Jamie at his HQ. It was so interesting and I had the greatest time – I didn't want it to end! Long story short, Jamie Oliver is literally THE BEST.

Love ya J!

Apple and blackberry, hazlenut and clotted cream loaf

- ♡ 150g unsalted butter
- ♡ 150g light brown soft sugar
- ♡ 3 eggs
- ♡ 185g self-raising flour (sifted)
- ♡ 1 tsp vanilla extract
- ♡ ½ tsp cinnamon
- ♡ ½ tsp baking powder
- ♡ 100g blanched hazelnuts, toasted and roughly chopped
- ♡ 300g Bramley apples (2 apples, peeled and chopped into cubes)
- ♡ 200g blackberries

ICING:

- ♡ A tub of clotted cream (approx. 200g)
- ♡ ½ tsp vanilla extract
- ♡ 150g icing sugar (sifted)
- ♡ 1 tbsp whole milk

METHOD

1 Preheat the oven to 180°C (Gas mark 4). Grease and line a 900g loaf tin with baking paper.

2 Beat butter and sugar together until well combined. Add eggs one at a time, beating after each one and adding a little bit of self-raising flour (a few spoonfuls) after each addition.

3 Add vanilla extract and mix. Stir the remaining flour through with baking powder and cinnamon and 80g of chopped hazelnuts. Fold in chopped apple until just combined.

4 Spoon one third of the mixture into the loaf tin, then add half of the blackberries. Add another third of mixture, followed by the remaining blackberries and finish off with last third of mixture.

5 Bake for about one hour or until a skewer inserted into the centre of the loaf comes out clean, but check the loaf after 40 minutes and cover with foil if browning too quickly.

6 Leave to cool in tin for 10 minutes before turning out to cool completely.

7 For the icing, whisk clotted cream until smooth and gradually add icing sugar until well combined. If too thick, add a little bit of milk (1–2 tsp) to loosen it. Keep the icing cool until the loaf has completely cooled and is ready to ice.

8 Cover the loaf with clotted cream icing and top with remaining hazelnuts. Lovely served with more blackberries.

Coconut and lime cupcakes for Nicole Scherzinger

Where do I start with Nicole? We have been able to share so many special moments together throughout the years. Like my interview with Jamie, I wasn't too nervous to interview Nicole Scherzinger. I first met Nicole back in November 2016, when I was given the opportunity to film a video with her for my channel. I'd actually had a nosebleed on the way to meet her and didn't feel 100%, so was feeling pretty anxious. But, as soon as I met her, she made me feel completely at ease and comfortable – I was just able to be myself. I brought two massive sketch pads along with me, so we chatted, doodled and laughed, A LOT.

I left on such a high and was so glad that I pushed myself to do it. She had such a calming and gentle presence. We were then reunited in 2017, which is when I properly interviewed her for "Nikki Lilly Meets". It was really, really lovely to see her! We talked about everything, from how she told Prince William she had a crush on him to how singing is her outlet to express herself. We ate lots of cupcakes and it was the best.

Me and Nicole!

Fast forward to 2018, Nicole did the sweetest thing for me. After she heard about my super-hard time in hospital, she wanted to visit but I was about to be discharged so I told her not to worry as she was very busy at the time. But she was insistent on seeing me and checking that I was OK so she ended up visiting me at home! She brought me a gorgeous bunch of flowers and a card – it TRULY made such a big difference to me mentally at the time and meant the world; she didn't have to do ANY of that. I could go on and on and on about just how incredible a person Nicole Scherzinger is, and all of the other things we have done together like speaking at WE DAY in 2019, hand in hand. But basically I love her loads and she has a heart of gold.

Coconut and lime cupcakes

CUPCAKES

- 175g caster sugar
- 175g softened butter
- 3 eggs
- 165g self-raising flour, sifted
- ½ tsp bicarbonate of soda
- Finely grated zest of 2 limes
- 3 tbsp coconut cream or milk
- 30g unsweetened toasted desiccated coconut
- 1.5 tbsp of freshly squeezed lime

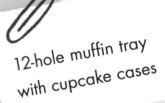

12-hole muffin tray
with cupcake cases

COCONUT AND LIME ICING

- 150g softened unsalted butter
- 300g icing sugar, sifted
- 2–3 tbsp coconut cream
- Finely grated zest of 1 lime
- 75g of toasted coconut curls or desiccated coconut to decorate
- Chocolate coconut bar (e.g. Bounty) sliced into small pieces

METHOD

1 Preheat the oven to 170–180°C or gas mark 5 and line a 12-hole muffin tray with cupcake cases.

2 Sift the self-raising flour into a large mixing bowl then add the bicarbonate of soda and caster sugar followed by the toasted unsweetened desiccated coconut and finely grated zest of two limes.

3 Add the softened unsalted butter to the bowl along with three eggs and beat everything together in a food processor on a medium speed for 1–2 minutes.

4 Next add the coconut cream mixing again for 30 seconds followed by the freshly squeezed lime juice and mix again for a few seconds.

5 Divide the mixture into the cupcake cases filling each case to two thirds full.

6 Bake in the oven for approximately 20–25 minutes or until golden and springy to the touch.

7 Allow to cool in the tin for a few minutes and then transfer to a rack to cool completely before icing.

8 To make the buttercream icing, beat the softened butter in a food processor until pale and fluffy.

9 Next add your sifted icing sugar to the butter in three parts, beating on a low speed after each addition then turning up the speed and beating until fully

incorporated. Add the coconut cream to the icing mixture — start with two tablespoons and add more if the mixture is too stiff. Beat again briefly then finally mix in the lime zest.

10 To decorate, spoon or pipe your buttercream icing onto your cupcakes; top with coconut curls/desiccated coconut and a slice of chocolate coconut bar in the middle.

Now it's your turn!

Is there something you'd really love to do, but you've let fear put you off? If so, for this chapter's challenge, why not give that thing a go and take just one small step towards achieving it. And, as always, don't forget to share it with me on social media. Don't worry, I'll be your biggest cheerleader!

#COMEONREADER

"Here's to sprinkling
kindness everywhere
we go."

CHAPTER NINE
Kill them with kindness

Kindness is SO, SO important to me, especially since I was diagnosed. As someone who looks different and who is in and out of hospital a lot, I appreciate other people's kindness so much more, especially if they don't even know me. The first couple of times I was in hospital, I felt very isolated. For long amounts of time I was barely at school or around people my own age and the only people I saw were my family or doctors and nurses. Obviously, it's part of a nurse's job description to be kind, but the nurses at my hospital always go above and beyond. Even though they were rushed off their feet, they would always make the time for a chat to ask me how I was feeling and to reassure me, which I really needed and appreciated. I can be such a chatterbox, so it was so nice to have someone else to talk to and it made me feel a lot less alone and more in touch with the outside world, even if I couldn't physically be there. That's when I first truly realized the power of kindness and what a lasting effect it can have. If you can be one thing in the world, be kind – plus it's free!

Because I've benefitted so much from other people's kind doings, when I started my channel it felt like a no-brainer to use it for good. Even when I only had one subscriber, I hoped my videos could have a positive effect on them and be a source of escapism. I think that if you have any kind of platform, then you should be using it to help in some way. If everyone did that the world would be a much better place. I know things are changing but I wish more celebrities would use their voice to help others. If they spoke more about notable things like body image or depression, I think people my age would be in a much better head space and feel less alone. In this chapter I'm going to share how kindness has helped me and how it can help you and others around you too...

Dani Dyer

Scarlett Moffatt

Jamie Oliver

Be kind to you

In one of my fave shows, "Ru Paul's Drag Race" (if you haven't watched it yet, um, what are you doing?), Ru Paul says: "If you can't love yourself, how are you gonna love somebody else?" It's exactly the same idea when it comes to kindness. If you aren't able to be kind to yourself you'll find it really hard to be kind to others. The trouble is, most people are really hard on themselves – myself included. I used to be seriously unkind to myself when I didn't do as well as I wanted to in school, I'd call myself stupid, incapable, lazy … the list goes on. And I was really mean to myself about my appearance too. For a few years, I had eating problems and I wasn't kind to myself at all. I'd call myself "fat" constantly and say mean things to myself like, "everyone thinks you're fat when they look at you." As a result, I wouldn't eat very much as that was the only way I could gain control. Then after getting some help, I gave myself a pep talk and said to myself, "Nikki, you need to be kind to yourself or you'll never be happy. If you don't help yourself, no one else can help you either."

The way I stopped being hard on myself about my relationship with eating was by speaking to people about how I was feeling. Opening up to others about how you're feeling is an act of kindness because it helps you get to the root of the problem.

> YOU NEED TO BUILD A BARRIER AGAINST BEING UNKIND TO YOURSELF. MAYBE WE NEED A NEW VITAMIN — VITAMIN K FOR KINDNESS — INSTRUCTIONS, TAKE ONE EVERY DAY!

If I don't do well in a school test now, I focus on the fact that I've missed lots of school, so it isn't a level playing field and I should still feel proud of myself. Now I try to see the positives rather than negatives and put things into perspective. And the more you choose to see the good and do good, the easier it becomes. I've also realized that everyone has times when they beat themselves up and feel bad, and knowing that has made me feel less alone.

Start your own movement

Being kind to others is the gift that keeps on giving.

> LITERALLY, EVERY TIME YOU DO SOMETHING
> KIND FOR SOMEONE ELSE, HOWEVER SMALL IT
> MIGHT BE, IT WILL MEAN MORE TO THAT PERSON
> THAN YOU WILL EVER KNOW.

Hopefully it won't just have a positive effect on them, but will inspire them to maybe do something kind too. Plus, you're bound to feel positive and proud of yourself too. An act of kindness doesn't have to be anything extravagant. A simple act of kindness can be just as rewarding, if not more. Some simple acts of kindness that I love doing are:

♡ Telling someone I don't know that I love what they're wearing (obvs, genuinely)

♡ Picking something up for someone if they drop it

♡ Giving someone my seat on a train.

Even if they don't seem to appreciate what I've done, I still feel content with myself for trying.

At school, make kindness all-inclusive

As we've already established, school can be a pretty stressful place at the best of times, so the more people who are kind in that environment, the better, as far as I'm concerned. My English teacher is lovely. Like the nurses, she goes above and beyond to show that she cares and has time for everyone, including me.

SHOWING THAT YOU'RE THERE FOR PEOPLE IS A HUGE GIFT THAT YOU CAN GIVE TO OTHERS.

She was so helpful all through last year, and gave me more confidence and support when I wasn't at school. She was the only teacher who would print out the power points and other resources from the lessons I'd missed.

157

And it was all out of kindness and thoughtfulness, as she didn't have to do any of it. I get so scared about falling behind at school, but my teacher would never be hard on me and would reassure me when I was apologetically telling her I'd have all the work that I had missed done by the end of the week. She'd say to me, "Nikki, honestly, just do the work when you can. As long as I know you're trying, it doesn't matter." She understood that I was in a different situation to the rest of my class and needed some extra time. And in spite of what I'd been through, and all the school I missed last year, I did really well in English.

Because of her kindness, when we had a teacher appreciation day last year, I made sure I took my time to write a little heartfelt message about what her kindness and dedication had meant to me. This is what I mean about the butterfly effect of kindness. Her being kind to me made me want to be kind to her.

At the end of the day, we're at school most of the time, so it makes total sense to try and create a really positive and welcoming environment through the power of kindness. There are so many ways to be kind at school; it doesn't have to be time-consuming or anything flashy. You could lend someone a pen, or give someone who has been off sick your notes and fill them in on what they've missed – this is so helpful for me! I appreciate anyone who has done this in the past. LITERAL. LIFESAVER. If I ever see someone who looks down or alone, or who has been bullied, I try to take the time to say hello to them or ask them how they're doing and if they're OK. You never know, even a simple smile could make such a positive impact on their day.

Save energy by being kind to your family

Being kind to my family is a huge thing for me because they're the people who support me no matter what, so it's really important to me that I show my appreciation. One time, when I was out shopping with my mum, she saw a cute necklace in a shop that she loved and showed me, but then followed it up with, "Oh no, I can't justify buying that." I knew that she really wanted it, so I bought it for her. It was the CUTEST surprise! But being kind to your family members doesn't have to cost a thing. It can be as simple as being a help around the house and loading the dishwasher. Or cleaning the toilet – if you're feeling really kind! Not sure I'm THAT kind though!

Even though I sometimes bicker with my family, especially my siblings – that's just unavoidable LOL – it's still super important to me to be kind to them too. For a start, I can never truly know what might be going on in their head or why they could be in a bad mood. However hard it might be, I try and put myself in their shoes and I don't let arguments drag on. My brother Alex is the most forgiving sibling and member of the family. If we ever bicker, he'll always be the one to end it with a hug. After an argument with my mum, I'll sometimes give her the silent treatment but then about half an hour or so later she'll come into my room and say, "Can we be friends again?" and we'll hug it out too.

THE FACT IS, IT TAKES A LOT OF ENERGY TO BE UNKIND AND LIFE IS TOO SHORT FOR GRUDGES.

Everyone gets into arguments, makes mistakes – we're all human at the end of the day. Apart from anything else, being kind saves energy and shows how much you appreciate those around you.

Make your comments online mindful

Being kind online is literally about being more mindful with your comments. There's so much negativity in the world and online, there's no way I'd ever want to add to it. It's so important to support each other. Even if I see something that makes me feel a bit jealous, I try to channel that energy into being nice rather than nasty. If I ever catch myself having a thought like, "Oh god, it's not fair! Why are they so good looking?" I remind myself that I don't know what might be going on in their head. For all I know, they could have all kinds of issues or insecurities. I always think that leaving a kind comment about someone's personality rather than their looks is a much more thoughtful thing to do and something they'll probably appreciate — more so than something superficial.

A THOUGHTFUL COMMENT LIKE, "YOU'RE SUCH A LOVELY PERSON!" WILL PROBABLY HAVE A MORE POWERFUL EFFECT THAN "OMG, YOU'RE SO PRETTY!" ON THE PERSON IN THE LONG TERM.

I'm so grateful for the kindness I receive online. I get such sweet comments and so much love which makes SUCH a positive difference to me, particularly on a bad day. YouTube can be like Marmite: either you love it or hate it. I hate it when I fall into the trap of comparing myself unfavourably to others. And whenever I post a video that doesn't do well it can be really disheartening – especially if I've put a lot of time and effort into it. But when I get a kind comment like, "I loved this video" or "your videos mean the world to me," it's such a nice feeling. So, if you've ever left a kind comment on one of my videos or posts, THANK YOU, I love you so, so much!

Me and fellow YouTubers campaigning to prevent cyberbullying #StopSpeakSupport

Sprinkle your work with kindness

I try to bring kindness into the work I do, too. Baking for each of the guests on my show "Nikki Lilly Meets" is one way that I do this and I love seeing their responses when I surprise them with their cakes. When I interviewed Jamie Oliver, I made him a blackberry and clotted cream apple loaf (see page 143). As you can imagine, it was SO nerve-wracking baking something for a world famous and incredibly talented cook (and when I say so nerve-wracking, I mean absolutely terrifying!). But his face instantly lit up when I gave it to him and he was so happy he actually got up on his feet and danced around while he was eating it! As a result, I felt so happy after and I was smiling so much my face actually hurt!

Kindness goes full circle. Another way that I try to be kind is by being there for my followers. On my YouTube and Instagram I always let my followers know that I'm there for them if they want to talk. To me this is all about returning their kindness, because if it wasn't for their love and support, I wouldn't have the courage to be doing all that I'm doing – like writing this book! I also frequently try to share positive and relatable quotes to, hopefully, help my followers feel less alone. I also support my fan pages, like and comment on as many photos and videos as I can. I always make an effort to reply to comments on my posts and DMs – although it can take a while to get through them all!

My biggest supporter – my mum!

Random acts of kindness

When you do something nice for someone with no reason other than to be kind, not expecting anything back, that's known as a random act of kindness. They are usually spur-of-the-moment things or it wouldn't be random, would it?! The first time I did a random act of kindness was when I was about seven and I was on holiday in Greece with my family. One day I saw a little girl who was sitting on the side of the street alone, begging. I was so upset thinking about someone my age with no family to look after her that it made me cry. I went back to my hotel room and picked out anything I could find to give to the little girl – a cuddly toy, a blanket, some money and some food and I put it all into a box. Unfortunately, when I went back to give it to her, she was no longer there which was upsetting, but I just had to hope that she was OK. My mum and dad were really proud of me for being so conscious of the fact that I was lucky to have a loving family and more. Another time, more recently, I saw someone – so talented – busking in a train station and instead of giving her some loose change (which is totally fine and every little helps) I put in a £20 note I received on my birthday from some family that I was planning to use to get a necklace. OMG, the look of surprise, gratitude and happiness on her face was so, so rewarding and made that £20 worth it.

Random acts of kindness don't have to be big, there are loads of opportunities to do them anytime and anywhere. One time, when my mum was paying for a car parking ticket, she realized that she was fifty pence short; the person behind us in the queue overheard and randomly (and very kindly) gave her the money. It was such a lovely thing to do and we really, really appreciated it – otherwise we couldn't have gone shopping!

ULTIMATELY, KINDNESS COMES IN ALL FORMS, SHAPES AND SIZES, BUT THE MAIN THING IS THAT A LITTLE BIT OF KINDNESS MAKES A BIG DIFFERENCE TO YOURSELF AND THE WORLD AROUND YOU.

Now it's your turn!

For this chapter's challenge, I'd like you to do something kind for yourself or for someone else. It can either be something I've suggested in this chapter or you can come up with your own idea. And, as always, make sure to tag me on social media as I'd love to see how you get on and what you did. Also, you never know, you could kick start a movement of kindness!

#COMEONREADER

Me, Tash and Alex

"Shoot for the moon.
Even if you miss, you'll
land among the stars."
Norman Vincent Peale